TWO-WEEK PIZZA PLAN

INCREASE YOUR PIZZERIA SALES BY $2000 IN JUST TWO WEEKS WITHOUT SPENDING A FORTUNE

by Richard Buchko

THE
TWO-WEEK
PIZZA PLAN

ISBN – 1440412995
EAN13 - 9781440412998

5th PRINTING – August 2012

©2008 Richard Buchko
All Rights Reserved – No part of this book may be
reproduced or copied in any manner without the
written permission of the author.   The knowledge
contained here can certainly be used – knowledge
cannot be copyrighted – but the book itself must be
respected.

Published by Richard Buchko
906-369-0793
historyandhobby@yahoo.com

INTRODUCTION

There are roughly 70,000 pizzerias of one type or another in the United States – that's one pizza place for every 4,250 people or so. I think the number is actually much higher, but since 94.3% of all statistics are wrong anyway (including that one), close enough. Pizza is an American cultural food, despite its Italian origins. The American pizza doesn't pretend, most of the time, to be old-world authentic. We know that someone from Italy would look at most of the pizzas made here and say, "What the Heck is this?" (although he'd most likely say it in Italian.) We don't care – most of us are not trying to copy what came over, we're trying to find what people want here and now. For those who seek authentic Italian pizza, that's great – you can find that, too. But this book isn't about how to make the best pizza, or where to find authentic Italian cuisine; This book is about how a pizza business in American today can make more money. Now, if that means making a superior pizza, so much the better – but we're going to talk about money, marketing, and creativity.

Whether you operate a single-store independent or manage one store in a 5,000-unit corporation, you'll find something in here that will help you make money. Obviously, the independents have more freedom to try new things, but at the end of the day there are simple, sound principles that lead to profits in this business.

As many learned the hard way, the pizza business is not easy. From the customer side of the counter it often looks easy, which is why most of the people who have called me over the years for marketing help share a similar story:

Mary and Linda were two sisters who were still young (30's & 40's), had a few dollars saved, and wanted to start a business. They saw an ad in the paper for a pizzeria that was for sale, and thought, "Let's open one of those – that seems easy enough." Six months later, doing $75 in sales on a Friday night, they were trying to decide whether or not to stay open.

Tony had been running a catering business in Florida for years, with good success. He had outgrown his existing building

3

and found another not far away that happened to have been a pizzeria at one point. He decided that since he was already a successful caterer, opening up the pizza place along with it would be a breeze. Certainly pizza had to be simpler than the complex dishes he prepared for his events, right? What Tony didn't take into account is that simple doesn't mean easy. The pizza business has the same headaches and problems all food service businesses do, the customers are completely different, and what works cooking for 64 people doesn't always work cooking for 6.

Throughout this book I'll mention some of the obvious advantages to the pizza business, including the different kind of customer relationship pizzerias enjoy when compared to other food businesses, the demand for the product, and the train-ability of making the product. Never confuse advantages or simplicity with *easy* – at no point will you read that the pizza business is easy. It's hard work, and frankly, most people don't do it all that well; but that's another advantage: Since most people are only so-so at best, with hard work, smarts, and some of the right information, you can increase your pizza profits!

This book will anger some pizza owners – it is inevitable. That's not something I enjoy; I want everyone to like me. Still, I'll be critical of ideas and practices that many stores currently use – and perhaps use successfully. Every store is different, and in order to make this information accessible to everyone I have to be general. So, for those who are offended by my words, I apologize.

I entered the world of pizza accidentally. I needed a job. Probably half or more of the people currently making pizzas, delivering pizzas, or running pizza stores got started the same way. Over the next 28 years I operated pizza stores, supervised training in multiple units, supervised the operations of dozens of units simultaneously, set-up training, wrote and produced training seminars and manuals, developed strategies and products – in short, I was lucky to see the good, the bad, and the ugly, from many different perspectives. I don't consider myself the do-all, see-all, end-all of pizza, but I have been fortunate to experience more than most, and this book comes from that experience.

I won't recount the history of pizza, either. Chances are the reader will know as much as I do about it, maybe more. It's worth pointing out, though, that pizza offers unique advantages when compared to other food service businesses, particularly the fast food world with which it is most often associated:

- ♣ More often than not, we are given the customers name, address, and phone number;
- ♣ We spend more time talking with each customer;
- ♣ Everyone likes the pizza guy!

But things have changed. There was a time in the pizza business when all you had to do to be successful was:

- ♣ Carry a decent product;
- ♣ Offer a decent value;
- ♣ Not kick the dog on your way to deliver the pizza.

Those days have long passed. Now it takes much more to maintain sales and profits, let alone to raise them. New challenges face the pizza storeowner today:

- ♣ Competition at every corner (pizza & other food);
- ♣ Changing eating habits and customer loyalties;
- ♣ Big chains spending millions on advertising;
- ♣ Employees demand more money while at the same time customers expect greater value;
- ♣ In many places the economy has changed and there aren't as many food dollars available;
- ♣ Costs have risen.

This is a challenging time.

You can't stop new businesses from popping up around you, you can't change the population, you certainly can't keep up with the advertising budgets of huge chains – and you shouldn't try! To raise sales and profits in this new market needs a different approach. You need something no one else is doing.

The pizza business isn't what it used to be, and neither should marketing be the same, yet the methods of attracting new customers in most cases haven't changed at all. In fact these methods have become less efficient, less valuable.

I have sales-building experience, in many environments, at many sales levels, and through careful study (and many failures) I've created a sales building system that can help you to raise your sales by as much as $2000/week – in just two weeks time. It's a low-cost approach, with high impact. You will:

- ♣ Find new customers;
- ♣ Find customers in new places;
- ♣ Get greater loyalty and higher ticket averages from current customers;
- ♣ Get back customers you lost.

I'm not simply going to tell you to send out as many pieces as you can, and I'm not going to tell you to discount to the bone to beat your competitor. In fact, most of the time I will tell you to send out fewer pieces (because it's not cost-per-piece that matters, it is response-per-piece), and often I won't advocate discounts at all. These methods are based on experimentation and obsession, on success and failure over the years. Along with years in the store making pizzas, I've spent the last few years concentrating on proving what does and doesn't work in different environments (urban, suburban, rural) and with different styles (carryout, delivery, dine-in). Along the way many ideas were proven, but some were changed. This book is the result.

Throughout this book I must refer to individuals, customers, employees, various people without names. Most of the time I will use the pronoun "he," for the sake of simplicity. It will be my coverall, but is not meant as a slight to women. I don't like the constant "he or she," "he/she," or "s/he" – so forgive me if there is any unintended slight.

Also, I will from time to time sound like I am commanding you – "Go, Do!" Most of the time this just means that I am confident in the value of what I am suggesting. I don't know your business and your people a tenth as well as you do, and I respect your business. Any impression that I am dictating is merely my enthusiasm for what I am talking about.

6

Finally, because I have spent so much time in the business and because much of what I write about is from first-hand usage, occasionally I'll talk in the first person and tell you what I do. This isn't ego, really – just telling you that I offer direct information, not something someone told someone who told someone.

This book is about marketing. There are some general operations tips, but more than anything this book is about what you can do, from a marketing perspective, to raise and retain sales

GOING FISHING?

Most pizza stores market like they are out fishing from a boat; they:

♣ Take the bait – that's the ad piece, usually a two-sided full color glossy sheet printed 25,000 at a time by a professional ad company (the *Mega-Ad*);

♣ Place it on the hook – the bulk mailer, the newspaper inset, the coupon-pack, etc.

♣ Throw out as many as they can afford (or the minimum these companies "allow" them to send);

♣ Hope for bites.

The fisherman has no specific target, and neither do most pizza owners. A fisherman is often happy to catch three or four fish after spending the entire day knee-deep in water, and if he later has to exaggerate the size of one of his catches, it's no big deal. The pizza store owner, though, won't be happy with just a new few customers out of a campaign, and no fantasy story will add money to his bottom line. Also, when the pizza store owner goes fishing, he loses the bait (it costs him money for each piece) whether he gets a bite or not.

Have you tried this method? Sure, sometimes you get bites from the sheer force of numbers, but does the increase in sales pay for what you spent **and** give you profit from it? A week later do these sales just seem to disappear?

The current popular form of fishing is bulk-distributed pieces by a third party, that *Mega-Ad* I spoke of. Usually it is the full-color two-sided glossy insert in the local paper or ad-pack, or a one-third sheet coupon in a mailed *Mega-pack* - or it's a box of flyers sitting under your counter, used for gluing onto pizza boxes..

The Mega-Ad salesman that visits your store will emphasize three important points: He'll tell you that the cost-per-piece is very low; He'll tell you that he can distribute thousands at once; and he'll tell you that studies prove the color photo flyers increase business by 20%. *These claims are usually true.* The cost per piece is low, but what good does that do you if the response rate is also low? He will distribute thousands, but again --- what's the response? Finally, while it is true that you'll get a 20% better response with the color, I'd ask 20% of what?

When full-color glossy inserts were unique, they worked better, but that was a long time ago. When you're in there with 3-5 other pizza stores, your ad doesn't stand out from the competitors, and it is going to be viewed by the customer, no matter now nice it looks, as "junk" mail, impersonal, you have to seriously ask if it is worth the hundreds of dollars it will cost.

The *Mega-Ads* are no longer the great sales-builder they used to be. For one thing, everybody uses them and they have become boring – they all look alike. If you have them inserted in the paper, or sent along with the latest coupon packs, ask:

- ♣ What is the response rate?
- ♣ How many are going to customers I already have, really just convincing some customers to spend less money?
- ♣ Do I know what day they are going to hit?
- ♣ Am I the only pizza place in there, or am I lumped in with 3-5 others?
- ♣ How do I know they all went out?
- ♣ How much did this cost, and what did I gain?
- ♣ Is it guaranteed to work?

It's not that I would never use this method. It has its place, and some stores do get really good results from it, but I wouldn't use it as my main method of marketing, and I wouldn't do it too often. A typical cost for *Mega-Ad* is $500-800*, it peaks quickly, and then the sales often disappear. These do very little to promote customer loyalty, or to set you apart from anyone else.

*Printing and delivery are charged separately by *Mega-Ad*, of course!

Worst of all, you often lose money when you use them! If you spend $500 to raise your sales by $500, you've lost money; even if you raise your sales $1000 by spending $500, because of food cost, labor cost, and your energy, you've still lost money. Yes, the pizza business is a long-term relationship and repeat business is the key, but this kind of *Mega-Advertising* doesn't promote loyalty, it doesn't promote multiple-purchases. This type of advertising, in most cases, attracts the coupon-cutters and TRANSIENT CUSTOMERS. If you spend $500, you need to make at least $1500 in increased sales to be profitable on those sales, and you need to have an advantage in bringing them back a second and third time.

The other problem with traditional pizza marketing is that it often uses just one piece to try to attract everyone. So, not only are most pizzerias fishing, they are trying to catch trout, catfish, carp, bass, and humpback whales all with the same bait! It would be great if this one-size-fits-all advertising worked – how much simpler it all would be! Sadly, it rarely works that way, not if you want the kind of business that encouraged you to buy this book. You have six types of customers, and each is looking for something different. One-size-fits-all doesn't work.

And forget about how hard you work at it – effort doesn't matter. In business if it doesn't work, doing nothing is cheaper.

Okay – enough about what doesn't work….. Now, about what *does work*.

I've seen the good, the bad, and the ugly – perhaps you have, too. I have seen people do terrific things to raise sales, and I have seen a lot of money wasted. My program eliminates the fat –the bad and the ugly – and allows you to raise your sales and profits at the same time, without spending a lot of money. Of course, this flies in the face of traditional advertising theory, which says that you have to spend money now, accept that it will cost more than you will initially receive in sales, and count on the long-term relationship of the pizza business to provide your profit. Hey, there's nothing wrong with that ---- if you've got a lot of money to spend on marketing, and if you've got the time to wait for the long-term relationship to pay off. I just don't think it is necessary, and many independent pizzerias don't have the time or the money to wait.

In the pizza market there is currently a large black book available which suggests ways to market your store. It has some terrific ideas. Some of them work, and some work very well. If you can ever find the book, it is worth reading; however:

- ♣ It doesn't give you a specific plan for your store.
- ♣ I costs $400. Or is it $600? For a loose-leaf book!
- ♣ It doesn't guarantee results.

Mine is not the only way to market your store – for some of you it might not even be the best way; however, if you're looking for a low-cost, high-impact method with immediate results, read on!

LET'S GO HUNTING

I described most pizza marketing as fishing. My program is more like hunting, CUSTOMER HUNTING. You have six types of customers and this is what you can do:

♣ Identify what customer type each person is, and go after him or her in the manner that he will best respond to. This means you'll get more responses from fewer pieces, saving you time and money in the end.

♣ Keep track of who responds and who doesn't; if one thing doesn't work, use other methods (never let them get away);

♣ Get customers to order more often, and to order a little bit more when they do (without even having to ask them).

It's a labor-intensive way of marketing; it takes work. If you don't have the time, most of it can be delegated to any intelligent person. Although it takes times and effort, the results are so much better than the fishing method that it's worth doing. With *Mega-Ad* you will be lucky to have an increase equal to what you spend on the ads, and you likely won't make any profit on them. With my program:

FOR EVERY DOLLAR YOU SPEND, YOU WILL GET A $5-10 INCREASE IN SALES IN TWO WEEKS, AND AT LEAST ANOTHER $5 IN THE THIRD WEEK.

That's right – up to $15 in increased sales in three weeks for a $1 cost. Imagine if you could get that kind of increase from *Mega-ad*! But you can't, and they won't guarantee any results at all! The only thing they will guarantee is that they will send it out, nothing about results.

Bold words from me, right? Okay, then – why does hunting work?

It works for many reasons, but chiefly because it is:

11

LAYERED – PROGRESSIVE – TIMED - TARGETED

It is layered - you don't just do one thing, wait until it wears off and then try something else; everything is happening at once. It's progressive – if one method doesn't work in attracting a customer, don't give up; try something different, or more aggressive. It is also timed – we know exactly when things will happen, when a customer will see a particular piece, and when you can expect to see results. Finally, as you keep hunting, each piece is targeted to a specific type of customer and designed to make that particular customer want to call you!

By letting multiple methods work at the same time – some requiring legwork and time, while other methods are off working on their own – you get faster results, with longer lasting effects. Unlike traditional marketing methods, it really never stops hitting.

As you know, the pizza business is cyclical – you have slower months and busier months, just as certain days of the week are always busier than others. You may have pay schedules in your community to contend with, events, and simply the unpredictable nature of people. There are always ups and downs, but we just try to keep the "downs" as small as possible while working on larger "ups".

YOU *WANT* COMPETITION

When speaking with pizzeria owners about competition, it is often one of the primary reasons stated for stagnant or sagging sales. To a point this is true – your competition does try to take away some of your sales, and they might be pizza stores or non-pizza stores. That's why they built the store, that's what they are designed to do. On the other hand, isn't that what you're designed to do, too?

If you have 15 competitors in your immediate area (typically a 2 mile radius if carry-out, as much as 5 miles around if delivery), and they have been there for a while, it tells you something --- it tells you that your area has the *ability to support* 15 businesses. Perhaps there are more – in many cases it can run into the hundreds.

The more competitors you have in your area, the better. Why? Because all you need to do is take a few customers from each, and you've increased your sales dramatically. If you have 15 competitors, and merely take ten customers from each in a week, you've increased your customer base by 150 people! Using a modest ticket average of $12, you've raised your weekly sales by $1800 ($93,600/year) - that's just taking 10 customers from 15 businesses. Could you take 20 a week from each? Maybe you have 30 or 40 competitors. If so, 20 customers from 40 competitors nets you a half-million dollars a year!

You're not putting anyone out of business, unless their sales are such that those 20 customers spell doom for them. I guarantee you they would be happy to take 20 from you.

Another reason competition is a good thing right now is the state of service in America. I'm not being a pessimist to point out that most businesses, most days, are not trying to impress anyone. *They are trying to service the greatest number of people spending the highest possible dollar amount in the fastest possible time with the fewest number of people at the lowest cost.* Many pizza shops, especially in major chains, make a point of doing just that day in and day out – I worked in chains

13

for over ten years, squeezing every drop of profit out of the sales that were there, wondering why I wasn't supposed to get more sales instead. Customers have come to expect a lower level of service and quality – and this opens the door for any business willing and able to work a little harder or a little smarter, to impress a customer and pull him away from competitors. While the guy down the street tries to do the least for the most, all you need to do is a little more than that guy down the street.

Will a little bit be enough?

In professional baseball, a hitter's batting average is his resume'. Far more than his character, his teamwork, or his understanding of the game, for most players the batting average is everything. Let's compare two batters, one with a so-so average of .250 and another with a very good average of .300. The .250 batter is barely going to be able to stay on the team, and while baseball players make obscene amounts of money, this guy is going to be stuck near the league minimum. The other guy, hitting .300 on a consistent basis, when his contract comes up is going to ask for, and probably receive, ten times as much money.

In the final analysis, though, how much better is he than the other hitter?

The difference between a .300 hitter and a .250 hitter is one extra hit every 4 ½ games.

That's right – a little less than twice a week the .300 hitter lines an extra one up the middle. The .250 hitter might be a better fielder, more loyal, a leader in the clubhouse, but that extra hit every 4 ½ games blows him out of the water.

Your competition, for the most part, is a team full of .250 hitters – large pizza chains with little desire to be innovative, burger and taco joints with procedures and policies that guarantee nothing special for the customer, and restaurants so concerned with cost percentages that they have forgotten where the profits come from. You don't need to be the best at everything; you just need to be a little bit better than them. You don't have to be 100% better at anything either – you don't need to shake up the world. Just be 1% better at whatever you do, and raising sales will come as naturally as opening the doors.

CADILLACS AND BICYCLES

Some car dealers have made a lot of money selling Cadillacs. Some salesmen make money selling bicycles. Did you ever see a dealer selling them side-by-side? No --- it would confuse people. You wouldn't see a salesman saying, "Well, if this $60,000 Cadillac doesn't appeal to you, how about this $120 bike?" There are Cadillac customers and there are bicycle customers. You wouldn't sell a Cadillac for a bicycle price – you'd go broke. You wouldn't try to sell a bicycle for a Cadillac price – no one would buy it, and you'd go broke.

It's no different with pizza. There are pizza stores that are successful because they can offer a great price. There are pizza stores that are successful because they make a high-end product for a high-end price. Other stores appeal to entertainment, variety of menu, or some other unique aspect or gimmick. Then there are the bulk of the pizza shops trying to market themselves as everything at the same time to a single customer, or shifting back and forth until no one knows what to think of them.

Why is McDonald's as successful as it is? Is it because they make the best burger in the land? Most would say no. McDonald's is as successful as it is because a Big Mac in Detroit tastes the same as a Big Mac in Butte, Montana or in Tallahassee, Florida. In short, people know what to expect.

In pizza, if you market yourself as a gourmet pizza shop, something worth paying a few bucks more to enjoy, then suddenly decide that you must compete with the $5 large pizza, and try to attract the same people who ordered gourmet pizzas, those customers will get confused. Your loyal customers will wonder if you compromised your standards. The $5-pizza customers will wonder what you did to make this "new" pizza so cheap. You'll lose your identity; you'll lose your customer base.

If you decide that you're a $5-pizza store, that's great. Be that, be proud, and be the best at it. Just don't be surprised when you have trouble selling your Chicken Cacciatore gourmet

15

pizza to $5-pizza customers. If you are a higher-priced pizza, you have to find reasons other than price to coax people to your store when the competition hires teenage kids to shake banners at passing traffic for their $5 pizza.

In either case, it is better to do one thing well than to fail on two fronts, because the old hunting proverb is true: *If you chase two rabbits, both will escape*. Recently I spent the afternoon with the owner of a 3-store pizza chain, and he was adamant that he could market effectively his Cadillac and his bicycle in the same ad. He argued this, while at the same time complaining that his sales were down 20% from last year. When I suggested that his Cadillac customers might regard the bicycle price as meaning he had compromised his quality, and that his bicycle customers might have thrown out the ad having only seen the Cadillac price, he felt I was being too critical. He was assuming that all people read and actually took the time to analyze his ads. They don't.

There are plenty of Cadillac customers and plenty of bicycle customers.

Does this mean you can't have the budget-priced pizza and the gourmet pizza both in your store, that you can't offer a good price *and* a good quality pizza? Of course it doesn't – variety of menu is often an advantage. It does mean, though, that you should only be marketing one type at a time to a given customer. An ad which features the $5 budget pizza next to the $20 gourmet pizza is not likely to be effective. A $5 sub alongside a $20 pizza is fine – variety of price point is often useful – but your pricing must make sense to the customer. Don't try to market both pizzas to the same customer; they will be uncertain what to think of you.

THESE POSTCARDS WERE USED IN A BUSINESS – FOCUSED MAILING. THE IDEA WAS TO HIT THEM WITH A DINNER IDEA BEFORE THEY WENT HOME, TO GIVE THEM REASONS TO READ THE CARD, AND TO SHARE IT WITH OTHERS. A SIMPLE GROUPS OF CARDS, NOTHING FANCY, BUT IN SOME AREAS THIS HAS BEEN VERY SUCCESSFUL. I'LL TALK A LOT MORE ABOUT POSTCARDS SHORTLY.

WHY DO PEOPLE BUY?

In any business that people can live without (and while we might not like to admit it, people can live without pizza just fine), your store needs something that sets it apart, a *Unique Selling Point* (USP). Like we've already seen in some examples, it can be just about anything (price, quality, entertainment, delivery, service, consistency), and it can be more than one thing, but something has to set you apart from the other guy, or there's little reason for customers to choose you over that other guy.

In the end – Cadillac or bicycle, why should someone buy from you? What is it about your store that is better (or different) than the next guy? It can be anything – but it has to be *something*.

When you boil it down and remove everything that doesn't matter, people buy for three reasons:

    1.   THEY NEED YOUR PRODUCT.
    2.   THEY WANT YOUR PRODUCT.
    3.   THEY LIKE THE SALESMAN.

That's it – there really is nothing more – and you can't rely on the first one. Any pizza store could close tomorrow and the world wouldn't stop spinning on its axis. People would still eat. Very little would change.

So that leaves the customer wanting your product – which involves their perception of value, personal taste, the objective quality of the product, and many other factors. We want them to want your product, and we go to great lengths to see that they do. The problem comes when you stop there and fail to realize that a lot of this is out of your control, including:

    ♣   PRICE – There will always be someone who can undercut you on price;
    ♣   ADVERTISING BUDGET – There will always be someone who can outspend you;

♣   CUSTOMER MOODS – You have no control over that;

♣   ROAD CONSTRUCTION – If they hate driving to you, you're at a disadvantage.

And much, much more.

Again, don't discount the importance of making the customers want your product – that's critical. Just don't rely on it. Remember that there are 4,538 other places trying to do the same thing. The best we can hope for, in many cases, is a tie.

Quality is not enough – because there are two types of quality:

OBJECTIVE QUALITY – THE DEGREE TO WHICH SOMETHING DOES WHAT IT IS SUPPOSED TO DO

If you put the key in the ignition and your car starts, the key has done its job, and must be considered to be of good quality. If you sit down to write a letter and the ink pen causes a line to form on the paper, it has done its job, and is of good quality. A football team knows that to be good, to win, at the end of the game they must have more points than the other team.

These are examples of objective quality, and it is important. However, another quality affects your sales every day:

SUBJECTIVE QUALITY – CAN BE JUDGED (FAIRLY OR UNFAIRLY) ONLY BY THE CUSTOMER

In the Olympics the Russian skater falls, but still gets a 9.0 score, and wins the gold medal. In college football the team that wins the Championship has a 11-1 record, but another team with a 12-0 record was never considered. In the grocery store a shopper sees a can of Del Monte corn that is 30¢ more than the store brand can of corn, but buys the Del Monte corn because it *must* be better (even though the shopper has tried neither brand).

Subjective quality often is based on things that have nothing to do with the true nature or value of a product or

19

situation, but each and every day your store, your pizza, is judge based on subjective criteria. The reason they want your product could be changed without you ever knowing. The rude phone person, the dirty apron, the half-lit sign – these all factor into the image of your store, and the taste of the pizza.

IN THE CUSTOMERS' EYES – TRUE QUALITY IS THE DIFFERENCE BETWEEN WHAT THEY RECEIVE AND WHAT THEY EXPECT

TAKE ADVANTAGE OF CUSTOMERS' LOW EXPECTATIONS – IT IS AN OPPORTUNITY TO IMPRESS

YOU ARE WHAT THE CUSTOMER THINKS YOU ARE

Of course, of the three reasons customers buy from you, that leaves only THEY LIKE THE SALESMAN, and this is where you must focus most of your energies. Friendly phone person, clean apron, fully-lit sign, these all become part of making them like you, but there is so much more. People want to feel good about who they order from, to whom they give their money. They want a sense of belonging; want to feel that your store is their place, a place where they can get "the usual" if they want – to steal the cliché, a place where everybody knows their name. Make them like you! Yes, price enters into is, but it will not be the determining factor, because as we've already said, someone will find a way to undercut your price. Make them believe you care about them (because you do), make them happy to see you, entertain, go the extra mile, do the little things like remembering and using their name, making small talk, show urgency.

When they sit down and decide where they are getting dinner tonight, even though they might be concerned about price, and they might be concerned about quality and convenience, the overriding factor that pushes them toward you or away from you is that they feel good ordering from you. If a lot of other factors in the objective category are equal or close - and usually they are - they'll order with their heart. That's why people drive farther, pay more, and wait longer, for businesses they like.

"Yes, everybody wants a good deal, but price is rarely the sole reason they decide to buy. After you've been to a restaurant, you don't remember exactly what the hamburger cost, you only remember whether you liked it or not.

"Besides, we can't compete solely on price. No matter what we charge, somebody -- because they're smarter (they figured out a way to be more efficient) or dumber (they don't really know what their costs are) -- can always charge a dollar less."

----- Carl Sewell, *Customers for Life*

Helping the customer to feel good about ordering from you, ordering more often, spending a little more, combines everything from price and value, atmosphere and entertainment, selection, convenience, perception of quality, cleanliness, and last but not at all least – what they think of your marketing.

Look at your marketing materials, side-by-side with the other guy's. Does your material tell the customer why they should buy from you? Does your material stand out? Is it different, or is it another version of what the other guy does? If you took off the names, addresses and phone numbers, which piece is best? Why? Forget which looks prettiest; which one will get the customer to try it? Why? Price? Size? Variety? Quality? Something you can't quite put your finger on?

All these are ideas are interesting, maybe even entertaining - they certainly are to me – but in the end you want to know how you can get more customers, get them to order more often, and get them to spend more money when they do. CUSTOMER HUNTING recognizes that to accomplish that, you have to look at your six types of customers, and approach (attack) them in a way that works *for that type*. You cannot use a one-size-fits-all method!

SO – WHAT TO DO?

CUSTOMER HUNTING takes work, it takes effort, it takes energy. It will require the full-time effort of someone, whether that is the store owner or someone he relies upon. It involves learning as much as you can about every customer, every address, every competitor, every business. It is not easy.

After saying this, I am often told that it wouldn't be worth the time or expense. Is it worth 40 hours a week if your sales increase by $2,000/week, and can grow from there? As to the expense, chances are you'll spend less than half on these methods than you did on the latest bulk-distributed Mega-ad.

YOU HAVE SIX BASIC TYPES OF CUSTOMERS

- ♣ **CURRENT CUSTOMERS**
  (THEY ORDER FROM YOU REGULARLY)
- ♣ **NON-CUSTOMERS**
  (THEY ORDER FROM YOU RARELY OR NOT AT ALL)

22

♣ **LOST CUSTOMERS**
(THEY USED TO ORDER, BUT DON'T ANY MORE)
♣ **BUSINESS CUSTOMERS**
(A DIFFERENT ANIMAL)
♣ **STUDENT CUSTOMERS**
(A TYPICALLY NEGLECTED GROUP)
♣ **TRANSIENT CUSTOMERS**
(THEY AREN'T LOYAL, THEY AREN'T EASY TO ATTRACT, BUT THERE ARE A LOT OF THEM!)

Each of these groups responds to a different type of ad, a different approach. If you're using a one-size-fits-all marketing plan, you're missing most of them or spending hundreds more than you need to. One size (as those of us who shop for clothes can attest) does not fit all. We're going to hunt them down, one-by-one, and raise your sales.

REMEMBER: BUY YOUR DIMES FOR A NICKEL – SELL YOUR NICKELS FOR A DIME

This means that - more than anything - you have to know what your costs actually are, and be sure you're making money on each item. To most pizza owners this will seem like a completely obvious statement, but at least 10% of the pizza store owners that read this book are selling items at a much higher cost than they think they are. A small percentage – perhaps 1-2% - are actually paying more for an item than they regularly sell it for! I'm not talking about a loss-leader item or something that is given for a special occasion or purpose, but a regular menu item or coupon item that the owner doesn't realize is costing more than he receives.

This book is not about pricing or operations, so my only comment will be to be sure --- look at all the numbers, and make sure that you are not selling your dimes for a nickel.

Now let's look at those six types, and the methods you can use to attract each type.

CURRENT CUSTOMERS

These people order from you on a regular or semi-regular basis. You can assume that, so far, they have been happy enough to keep ordering from you. Some are long-time customers and others may be recent acquisitions. Theoretically you shouldn't have to do anything more to keep these customers than to make sure that you give them what they want when they call. *Theoretically*. The reality is that these customers are being constantly exposed to other options, that they sometimes get bored after a while and would never mention it, and that in your store things might not always go perfectly. Just because you have them doesn't mean you won't lose them. As I wrote at the start of this book, keeping customers is a lot more difficult than it used to be. Let me put it this way: If your sales are down from last year or the year before, you have lost people.

In addition to keeping them as customers, you would also like to:

❑　　　When they order, coax them to order more often
❑　　　When they order, encourage them to order a little bit more

FOR THE PURPOSE OF EXAMPLE, WE'RE GOING TO USE A $12 TICKET AVERAGE. YOURS COULD BE MUCH HIGHER OR LOWER, BUT THIS REFLECTS A NATIONWIDE AVERAGE FOR PIZZA.

TWO-TIMER CARDS

On the busy weekend nights (Friday-Saturday or Friday-Sunday) you will see most of your customers; often that's the only time you see them. If you can get some of them to order again on the slower days you'll make more money with the same customer base. TWO-TIMER cards are simple, low-cost ways to coax them in a little more often – just by sending one out with every weekend order. They can be business card sized or postcard sized, with a very modest offer (usually a free topping, bread or drink) if they order again within a few days. Most of them just get put up on the refrigerator, slapped on with a magnet. The short expiration date and the simple offer will make some people think of your store when they consider their weekday dinners. It's a non-intrusive method of marketing. The response is usually 3-5%, which isn't high, but TWO-TIMER CARDS cost next to nothing. If you send out 200 over the course of a weekend, and get 9 back, you've still raised your sales by $108, doing very little.

As you use other methods to increase your sales, TWO-TIMER CARDS will be given to new customers, so it will take a while for the novelty to wear off. I recommend a different card/offer every 3-4 weeks to maintain newness.

BENEFITS OF TWO TIMER CARDS:

- ❑ BUILD SALES W/ CURRENT CUSTOMERS
- ❑ NON-INTRUSIVE
- ❑ VERY LOW COST
- ❑ 3-5% RESPONSE

COST: $10-20 [NOTE: Throughout the book I will give you approximate costs, but your exact cost will depend on your method of printing and the style of piece.]

RESULTS: Although TWO-TIMER cards will cause 3-5% of your customers to order more often or more quickly, we don't have any way of knowing what they would have done, so there is no way to measuring this with great accuracy. Still, if 3% of your customers order twice/week instead of their usual once/week, that's profit!

STEP-UP CARDS

Getting them in the door more often is great. Getting them to order just a bit more is even better. With every order during the slower days (when you're not sending a TWO-TIMER CARD) you send out a STEP-UP CARD. If they order a small pizza you send a card that features a medium pizza. If they order a medium you send one which features a large, and so on. If you want them to try new items, your card could offer a non-pizza item of slightly higher cost. Like the TWO-TIMER CARDS many don't get saved and most don't get used, but if you can get 3-5% of the people to step up to the next size, you'll be making more money without any extra effort.

Training a customer to want a little more is a long-proven method of marketing, but not commonly used in pizza marketing. When that customer realizes he *likes* having more, or that he *likes* having leftovers, he'll do it all the time.

The reason we use these on the slower days and the one-style TWO TIMER CARDS on the weekends is that a little more time (a few seconds) must be taken to decide which is the right card to use.

BENEFITS OF STEP-UP CARDS:

- ❑   BUILD SALES WITH EXISTING ORDERS
- ❑   NON-INTRUSIVE
- ❑   VERY LOW COST
- ❑   3-5% RESPONSE

COST: STEP-UP CARDS - $10-20

RESULTS: Like the TWO-TIMER CARDS, these are going to people who already bring you money. The STEP-UP to the next size can be measured, but how this will translate into sales cannot, so we enjoy the increase and the low cost, but it's not included in the results total later in the book.

CURRENT CUSTOMER SURVEYS

If someone orders from you regularly you assume they're satisfied with your product and service. But do they know everything you have to offer?   Could there be an underlying problem which hasn't yet caused them to go elsewhere, but which leaves you vulnerable to something the competition might offer? I recommend that you send out at least 100 surveys to CURRENT CUSTOMERS so you can get a picture of how your customer base perceives you. If 6 people out of 100 say that Johnny's delivery-car radio is too loud, you can bet that other customers (and even NON-CUSTOMERS) thought so, too. Not every opinion is valid (despite the traditional saying, the customer is *not* always right), but you could find patterns that lead to answers. These don't translate into immediate sales increases, but can often alert you to issues which are costing you other customers – and if a survey customer has a problem in the future, he is more likely to come to you as a friend instead of an adversary because he knows you care – after all, you asked his opinion.

(SEE THE SECTION "WHY YOU NEED TO DO CUSTOMER SURVEYS")

BENEFITS OF SURVEYS:

- ❏ BUILD CUSTOMER LOYALTY
- ❏ TEACH YOU ABOUT THEIR PERCEPTIONS
- ❏ PROTECT AGAINST FUTURE PROBLEMS
- ❏ RESPONSE RATE 5-10%

COST: SURVEYS - $5-15
POSTAGE AND SUPPLIES - $40
LABOR – Can be integrated into a typical workday.

RESULTS – Again, these are CURRENT CUSTOMERS, so we're not including this in the results total. Because of the postage costs, owners are often tempted to skip this method altogether, or to instead boxtop surveys. You certainly can boxtop surveys, but your customers are not going to be impressed by it; they are not going to think of you as contacting them personally. In short, while you'll still get the information, the other benefits will not be there.

28

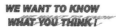

WE WANT TO KNOW WHAT YOU THINK !

Hello!

At PIZZA SOCIETY we want to be *your* pizza shop. You can help us serve you better by letting us know about your PIZZA-BUYING habits.

If you'll give us a try we're sure you'll agree that our PIZZAS, SUBS, DINNERS, AND other terrific items are the best in town – and a great value! As a THANK-YOU for taking the time, we want to give you this special certificate.

Try us --- we believe you'll come back again and again.

YOUR FRIENDS AT PIZZA SOCIETY

NON-CUSTOMERS

These are people who don't order from you at all, or very rarely. Chances are they get whatever ad piece you send out, but haven't responded. This is the largest group in your area. You need to reach them, but whatever you are doing now isn't working as well as you need it to.

One of the reasons you aren't reaching enough people is that you're trying to reach too many people. Instead of trying to expose 10,000 people to your store and hoping that 1% try you this month, my program only targets about 3,000 people at a time - but we target them effectively and we don't give up.

No ad piece is effective with everyone. Different people respond to different things, and a little later on in this book I talk about that in detail. What you're looking for, though, is something simple, effective, and easy to track.

NON-CUSTOMER SURVEYS

Even though these people haven't tried your store, they have probably been to some pizza store, and you can benefit from finding out what they liked – or didn't like. When you ask someone their opinion you give them a reason to like you, and as we've said, *people want to order from people they like*. Often just asking their opinion is enough to get them to try your store, although we send an offer along to give them a nudge. The response is typically 5-10% because you have created some *instant loyalty* by asking their opinion.

You'll survey two different ways: you'll mail out surveys to (100) non-customers, sending with it an offer to help entice them to try your store. The offer can be very conservative or very aggressive – but it is usually the survey that brings them in.

The second method is DOOR-TO-DOOR SURVEYING. Start walking house-by-house in areas of weaker sales, knocking on the doors and asking a few pizza-related questions. For their time, offer one of three different free item cards:

- ♣ FREE BREADSTICKS or other small item for those who are current customers;
- ♣ FREE PIZZA for non-customers or those who have been dissatisfied;
- ♣ SOMETHING DIFFERENT to address specific questions or for non-pizza eaters.

Over a two-week period you can visit at least 120 houses (2 hrs X 5 days X 6 houses per hour). During Week One the houses are chosen at random in areas where you perceive weaker sales. During Week Two you'll be targeting specific houses, based on information we'll talk about shortly.

THE BENEFITS OF NON-CUSTOMER SURVEYS:

INEXPENSIVE – The only significant cost is food.

PERSONAL – The potential customers react favorably to someone asking their opinion and to getting something free.
EFFECTIVE – Not only builds customer loyalty, but also most customers will add to their "free" order.
RESPONSE RATE 5-10% (MAILED); 15-30% (DOOR-TO-DOOR)

COST: SURVEYS (100 TO BE MAILED) - $5-10
POSTAGE AND SUPPLIES - $40

RESULTS: $396-792 INCREASED SALES

At this point you might be saying, "Wait a minute! Are you telling me that I have to spend 20 hours going door-to-door?!?"

No, not really. You don't have to. You could:

- ♣ Mail all 220 instead of 100 (add $50 to cost);
- ♣ Have someone else do it (add $140 to cost);
- ♣ Ignore this altogether (you won't get the $396-792 in sales increase);
- ♣ Call me on the phone and yell at me.

This is worth doing! The 15-30% return is conservative; stores often do better. The new customers, the information you gain about your store image, the LOST CUSTOMERS you get back, all make it worthwhile. Remember, the $396-792 increase is just the first two weeks. Between residual effects of late-responders and the repeat business from the people you have hooked, those 20 hours will net you $20,000/year or more. I think $1000 return for each hour invested is good, don't you?

WHY YOU NEED TO DO CUSTOMER SURVEYS

#1 -YOU CAN'T SUCCEED BY GIVING THE CUSTOMER WHAT HE EXPECTS

#2 – UNTIL YOU KNOW WHY SALES ARE LAGGING, IT IS IMPOSSIBLE TO CORRECT THE PROBLEM.

LOOKING AROUND THE STORE IS NOT GOING TO BE ENOUGH. THE PEOPLE WHO KNOW WHY YOU ARE SUCCESSFUL OR NOT ARE YOUR CUSTOMERS – ASK THEM.

It only seems logical that the key to success, in any business, is to meet the customers' expectations – and I have already said that customers have, in general, low expectations (based on multiple bad experiences at many places in the past). Still, striving to meet their expectations will often doom you to failure because:

♣ You have no idea what they expect;
♣ Their expectations will change over time.

Tomorrow when you open your doors, do you know what the customer is looking for? Do you know what they see when they come into your store? What factors are important to them, and which aren't? Most pizza owners, most of the time, don't know. You could be the exception, and if so, more power to you. If you already know how your customers perceive you, whether they see you as selling Cadillacs or bicycles or something else, whether they are happy with you or not, terrific – you're on your way to much greater sales. However, the history of business is filled with the assumption of what customers want, leading to terrific failures. Every year hundreds of movies totaling billions of dollars in production costs reach the theaters with high expectations, only to have people show no interest at all (remember *Ishtar*?). On the other hand, a small independent film costing next to nothing relative to other films, becomes a runaway hit (*Blair Witch Project* – cost a few thousand, made millions). Books, TV shows, songs, and countless other products reach the consumer with expectation of success, and fail.

One company about 25 years ago did marketing research that indicated a particular product would be successful. They "knew" it was time for something different, and "knew" people wanted it. This company spent billions of dollars to produce the new product instead of the old one, spent millions to market it —

and lost those dollars when the public didn't want their changes, forcing them to drop the product and bring back what they originally sold. The company was so certain of the success of *New Coke* that they were stunned by its failure. There was no intention to bring back what was called, for years after, *Classic Coke*, but that's what people wanted.

So, what does this mean? Are we at the mercy of the whims of the public? Should we just give up?

Of course not --- although we'll never anticipate every need, never satisfy every customer, and from time to time will have a miserable failure, you can be successful by doing three things:

♣ Find out what your customers think – every day;
♣ Don't try to meet their expectations – try to exceed them;
♣ Assume everything is important.

That first step is to do the surveys --- informal surveys through everyday conversation, phone surveys by asking simple and quick questions when they call, and more formal written surveys like those outlined in this booklet. You will get some conflicting information, you'll find that some people have opinions which to you don't make much sense, but over a very short time you'll find patterns, and you'll see how your customers perceive you.

Once you have that information, you must go to work exceeding those expectations, and where necessary changing those opinions. If your store is perceived as dirty (even if you don't think so) break out the scrubbers and the paint. If you're perceived as rude or indifferent, become the friendliest place in the city. If you are perceived poorly because the previous owners made a disaster out of your customer base, do what you need to do: change your name if necessary.

Finally, although you will prioritize the opinions according to common sense, realize that the customers will change their priorities without telling you, so assume that everything is important, and act on it where you can.

Easier said than done, but better to do than to lose customers.

If you don't do surveys and people are unhappy:

♣ 96% of dissatisfied customers don't say anything;
♣ 91% of those people never come back.

So, if you wait for complaints to come to you, each one that you hear means there is a strong likelihood that nine other people thought the same thing, and most of them just never came back - without saying a word.

You might get few complaints – maybe you get none. Your customers could be thrilled. That's fantastic; it's what we all want in business. If your sales are not increasing dramatically, though, there is a reason. You can use just trial-and-error marketing methods, just go fishing, and hope; or you can go right to the people who make those decisions and ask them.

POSTCARDS

I love this method! Use POSTCARDS in a limited mailing. The process is:

❀ Create 4-8 different cards;
❀ Using the local phone book, grab addresses in your area at random (if you have customer records, don't send to CURRENT CUSTOMERS);
❀ Mail 300 the first week (50 of each type);
❀ Track the cards which get the best response;
❀ During the second week mail another 300, but only those cards which got a good response (100 X 3, 150 X 2, or maybe 300 of the best card!).

The POSTCARDS are focused in these areas:

34

❑ The area right around your store, because you can service these people easily and should have them.
❑ The area right around your competitor's store, because HE can service them too easily.
❑ Any areas where you see weak sales (see "SECTOR ANALYSIS").

POSTCARDS get about a 10% response, sometimes a bit higher. Typically I'll make some with lower price points, some in the mid-range, and then some higher, and watch what comes back before making the second wave – seeing whether you are perceived as a Cadillac dealer or a bicycle dealer, seeing what people want to buy, seeing what the right product mix is or magic words are that will bring the customer to your door. That is the great beauty of POSTCARDS – you can change them at a moment's notice to whatever is working, whatever you want to try. Not sure whether your "Family Deal" should be $15.95 or $16.95? Send out 50 of each and see which card comes back more often. If the more expensive card comes back just as often (or close enough), it could mean that you don't have to knock off the extra buck, that people perceive the higher price as a good value. Most of the time, since they are going to people who have never ordered from you before, I wouldn't even discount – the cards simply highlight regular prices or regular coupons you already use.

THE ARGUMENT *AGAINST* POSTCARDS

Many pizza shops don't like the idea of postcards. It's the hardest idea to sell them on. They want to show the customer their variety of menu, and feel that the more choices they give, the greater the chance that something will appeal to the potential customer.

The problem is that you have most likely used this show-them-everything method, and it hasn't worked as well as you want it to. Everyone is sending them menus; everyone is inundating them with information. People want choices, but not *too many* choices. It's no insult to the average person to say that they are easily confused; offer people choices, but *limited choices*. Many people, when it comes time to make the food choice, if they don't have a pizza shop already in mind, go to the "coupon pile." If you have 500 items to wade through on your menu, it becomes a disadvantage. If, on the other hand, you have two or three GOOD choices available on a card that stands out, one will be more likely to catch his eye. Later, once they have reason to like you and are searching for variety, your full menu will be useful.

Get them to try you first.

Every store should have that USP - unique selling point. Whatever yours is, a postcard is the perfect chance to show it off!

When the first wave of postcards comes in, adjust the second wave so the offers that worked best are used most, and any card that didn't work is changed or scrapped.

Finally, anyone who doesn't respond to the postcard goes on the DOOR-TO-DOOR SURVEY list for the second week - we don't let them get away! If the postcard wasn't enough, the DOOR-TO-DOOR SURVEY might be.

NOTE: Did you know that most stamp dealers (yes, there are still stamp collectors and stamp dealers around) offer postage at a discount? Depending on location and what you need, you can buy your postage 80-90% of face value, saving you money. It's not as easy as going to the post office, but saving $28.80 on the mailing in this program might be worth it to you – it would to me.

WHY I DON'T SUGGEST A
LARGER POSTCARD MAILING:

We don't know which cards are going to work the best, or what the final response rate for each card will be. POSTCARDS, while a great way to market, even with discount postage, isn't cheap.

After the 2-week program, with the postcard return info, the survey info, and seeing what areas of the city respond to you the best, you might want to do a large postcard mailing (1000-2000 cards). The cost, even with discount postage works out to about 21-35¢ per card, which isn't cheap, and ***that's why we wait until we know what will happen***. If it's making you money, that's great, and maybe you'll want to try it. If it's not, there's no sense pouring money into it. ***LET'S FIND OUT FIRST.***

You can save money on POSTCARDS (and all mailing) by using BULK MAIL, but I hate it. With first-class mail you can mail on a Tuesday and know it will reach most of the homes on a Wednesday, you can mail as few or as many as you like, you can mail different pieces at the same time ---- and people can tell the difference between regular and bulk mail. If it's going to work, it is worth the extra few pennies per piece. If it's not going to work, there's no point in doing it.

THE BENEFITS OF POSTCARDS:

- ♣ EASY TO MAKE CHANGES
- ♣ CAN PRINT AS FEW / AS MANY AS NEEDED
- ♣ TREATED LIKE 1st CLASS MAIL – NOT JUNK
- ♣ YOU KNOW WHEN THEY WILL "HIT"
- ♣ EVEN IF THEY ARRIVE WITH OTHER ADS, THEY ARE ALONE
- ♣ THEY OFFER CHOICES, BUT KEEP IT SIMPLE
- ♣ YOU CAN TEST DIFFERENT PRICE POINTS FOR THE SAME PRODUCT IN DIFFERENT AREAS
- ♣ NO ONE ELSE IS DOING IT
- ♣ HUNT IN SPECIFIC AREAS
- ♣ AROUND YOUR STORE
- ♣ AROUND COMPETITORS STORES
- ♣ WEAK AREAS
- ♣ CAN USE MULTIPLE OFFERS (4-8 IS COMMON)
- ♣ CAN GEAR TO SPECIFIC CUSTOMERS
- ♣ CAN EXPERIMENT AND QUICKLY CHANGE
- ♣ STANDS OUT FROM BULK MARKETING
- ♣ RESPONSE RATE - 10%

COST: PRINTING - $18-36
         POSTAGE - $144

RESULTS: Approximately $720 in two weeks (If you keep only 50% of them as once-a-week customers, that's $18,720/year increase). It's a higher cost-per-response than other methods, but these are all NON-CUSTOMERS, so every sale is an increase!

DOORHANGING

Frankly, I hate doing this; it's boring, but it is very useful and cost-effective. To mail 5,000 postcards would cost over $1,000, but the same number can be taken door-to-door for just a few dollars. So, wherever and whenever logical, I do doorhanging. I don't worry about whether I am duplicating some of the NON-CUSTOMERS who received postcards because you really do want people to get multiple pieces (see "WHY YOU NEED MULTIPLE MARKETING METHODS" later in this book). How much you do simply depends on time. It gets a 3-5% return rate, which is good considering how little it costs compared to other methods. If you doorhang often, just make sure you use different pieces each time you hit the same area. Nothing gets tuned out faster than something they have seen before.

Yes, this is random - it is fishing; but there are times of the day and days of the week when it is the only worthwhile thing to do. Visiting businesses or knocking on doors for surveys on a Sunday morning wouldn't work – and there won't be any mail taking your pieces that day either. Doorhanging 1000 pieces a week takes a few hours.

THE BENEFITS OF DOORHANGING

- ❏ YOU CONTROL WHERE THEY GO
- ❏ YOU CONTROL WHEN THEY GO
- ❏ YOU CAN BE SURE THEY GOT THERE
- ❏ IT COSTS VERY LITTLE
- ❏ IF YOU HAVE A GOOD PIECE IT CAN BE VERY EFFECTIVE
- ❏ RESPONSE 3-5%

39

COST: $30-40

RESULTS: $360-600 IN 2 WEEKS

If you're a delivery store taking 125 deliveries a week, have the driver take two extra pieces on each delivery and drop one off at the houses on each side of the delivery. That puts 250 pieces a week out there, costs nothing but a few minutes here and there, and your customer base will expand naturally.

LOST CUSTOMERS

As the name suggests, these are people who used to bring you money but don't any more. There are plenty of reasons why they might have gone elsewhere:

- ♣ 3% MOVE
- ♣ 5% DEVELOP OTHER FRIENDSHIPS (WHO HAVE DIFFERENT FOOD LOYALTIES)
- ♣ 9% LEAVE FOR COMPETITIVE REASONS (PRICE, DIET, ETC.)
- ♣ 14% WERE DISSATISFIED WITH PRODUCT
- ♣ 68% PERCEIVED AN ATTITUDE OF INDIFFERENCE FROM YOUR PEOPLE!

You won't know the reasons right away, but it doesn't matter – you want them back! It is critical to be very aggressive with lost customers; they used to bring you money, and now they don't.

There are still pizza owners who subscribe to the myth that if you lose a customer, there's another one to be gained later on. Sure, there are more customers in your area than you can probably ever reach, but:

- ♣ The typical dissatisfied customer tells 8-10 people, and 1/5 will tell as many as 20!
- ♣ The average business spends 6X the amount to attract new customers as it would to keep old ones.

So, one unhappy customer could cost you 20 others, and just to get them back you would need to spend 6X the amount it cost to satisfy them. That alone should make you run for your records to find out who used to bring you money, but no longer does.

The best reason, though, to bring them back can be found by looking at how many LOST CUSTOMERS you have. Most stores that have been in business for a couple years have as many LOST CUSTOMERS as they have CURRENT

CUSTOMERS, often many more! Can you imagine your sales if you brought back just a fraction of those LOST CUSTOMERS?

LOST CUSTOMER LETTERS

Everyone who hasn't ordered from you within the last two weeks is a lost customer. Some pizza stores use 30 days as the cutoff, but I think that is risking losing them forever. A LOST CUSTOMER LETTER is very direct, and tells them exactly why you are writing – you want them back. The offer runs from mild (free topping) to aggressive (free pizza), depending on the store, the number of lost customers, and your profit goals. The way I look at it, if it costs you a pizza to get them back, it is worth doing. Every LOST CUSTOMER LETTER has a built-in survey (similar to the sample on page 30), which not only gives you valuable information, but also adds that extra reason for the customer to give you another chance – because you took the time and effort to ask their opinion. Send out at least (200) LOST CUSTOMER LETTERS. If you don't have that many, the letters go to NON-CUSTOMERS. If you have more, deliver the excess door-to-door so costs can stay reasonable. The response rate varies wildly, based on their reasons for leaving you, but can be 20% and more.

LOST CUSTOMERS who don't respond to the letter get a second, more aggressive offer, or visit them during week #2 with a DOOR-TO-DOOR SURVEY --- either way you hit everyone who got LOST, at least twice if needs be.

If you don't keep a record of orders you won't know who your LOST CUSTOMERS are. In this case you should send out more NON-CUSTOMER surveys to compensate – and then start keeping records!

THE BENEFITS OF LOST CUSTOMER LETTERS
- ❑ GREATEST SOURCE OF SALES INCREASES AMONG RESIDENTS
- ❑ PROTECTS AGAINST FUTURE PROBLEMS
- ❑ RESPONSE RATE 10-20% (SOMETIMES HIGHER - DEPENDS ON AGGRESSIVENESS)

COST: PRINTING - $10
      POSTAGE - $78

RESULTS: $540 IN THE TWO WEEKS – OR MORE!

BUSINESS CUSTOMERS

Your business customers are different from all the others in a few ways:

- ♣ Many don't live in your area;
- ♣ They order out more often, even every day;
- ♣ Time is always an issue;
- ♣ They talk about their food choices with more people;
- ♣ Variety is critical because they order more often.

They are different, so you have to treat them differently:

BUSINESS WALKS

Go to every business in your area, taking ad pieces and making sure they know who you are, and what you can offer them. Of all the methods, this gets *the best response*. Businesses often have many people looking for meals, they often order as a group, and because of the hectic nature of what they do you can gain their loyalty simply by making it easy for them. When I stop in to many businesses they are thrilled to see me; they have been "trying to think of something new;" they're tired of the place they use now, or mad at them, or just want variety. I invite them, and many respond. In a two-week span you can hit about 1200 businesses, depending on how spread apart they sit and the time you spend.

ALSO --- for every $100 in business customer sales you gain, you get another $30 in residential sales. People take the pieces home with them, and remember the conversation they had earlier in the day. It also often results in large catering orders. Businesspeople usually like me, and I use that to every advantage – you can, too.

A cool reception doesn't mean you haven't been successful. Many times I've visited a business and received a cold shoulder, only to find them ordering within a few days.

This is an exception to the simple-choice philosophy. For businesses, because of the number of people involved and their quirks, you definitely *want* the full menu to be a part of the package.

Another thing a good BUSINESS WALK piece will do is call attention – loudly – to your ability to handle large orders. Most menus have a little blurb somewhere, usually at the bottom, usually on the back, saying, "We Do Catering." ZZZZZzzzzzzzzzz You want large orders? Scream it out! A 4-page menu with the back page completely devoted to large orders, announcing it with pride and excitement, is an effective way to build your sales.

If you have a catering menu, hand these out on your BUSINESS WALKS. On more than one occasion I have completed my BUSINESS WALKS for the day, and on returning to the store found that a $300 order for that night had already been placed. Sometimes it was simple luck, being in the right place just when someone had a decision to make, but that's sometimes what it takes.

For lunch, visiting businesses from 9am-1pm is ideal, because you catch them before decisions have been made for the day regarding lunch. If you're not open for lunch, visit them from 1pm-5pm.

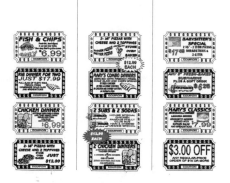

46

PIZZA

	12"	16"	18"	24"
Cheese	$3.00	$5.00	$8.00	$14.00
Toppings	1.25	1.25	2.00	2.00

TOPPINGS

EXTRA CHEESE, GREEN PEPPERS, HAM, CHICKEN,
MUSHROOMS, SAUSAGE, PINEAPPLE, ONIONS,
TOMATOES, PEPPER RINGS, FETA CHEESE,
PEPPERONI, BACON, BLACK OLIVES

DELUXE

PEPPERONI, HAM, BACON, MUSHROOMS, ONIONS,
GREEN PEPPERS, OLIVES, PEPPER RINGS

16" — $15.00   18" — $18.00

MEAT LOVERS

PEPPERONI, HAM, BACON, SAUSAGE

16" — $10.00   18" — $15.00

VEGGIE DELIGHT

MUSHROOMS, ONIONS, GREEN PEPPER, BLACK
OLIVES, PEPPER RINGS, TOMATOES

16" — $15.00   18" — $18.00

APPETIZERS & SIDES ITEMS

Soup Of The Day................................ 2.75
All Soups are made from scratch daily.
DAY OF THE WEEK - CHOOSE ONE DAILY

TUESDAY - HEARTY BEEF VEGETABLE
WEDNESDAY - CREAM OF POTATO
THURSDAY - BEAN WITH HAM
FRIDAY - CLAM CHOWDER
SATURDAY - CREAM OF BROCCOLI
SUNDAY - CABBAGE

Hearty Beef Stew................................ 3.25
IN A BREAD BOWL - $4.03
Homemade Chili................................ 3.25
IN A BREAD BOWL - $4.03
Breadsticks................................ 2.50
Freshly baked, WITH CHEESE
French Fries................................ 1.50
Chili Fries................................ 2.50
Chili Cheese Fries................................ 3.00

HOT OFF THE GRILL

Flame Grilled Burger................................ 2.25
WITH FRIES AND SODA - $4.50
ADD CHEESE, BACON, SAUCE OR MUSHROOMS OR JALAPENO
PEPPERS - .25 EACH
Grilled Patty Melt................................ 2.75
On Rye with Onion and choice of Cheese

GARDEN FRESH SALADS

Garden Salad................................ 3.50
Family Size (serves 4)................................ 7.00
Chef Salad................................ 5.25
Turkey Chef Salad................................ 5.25
Greek Salad................................ 4.25
Chicken Greek Salad................................ 5.25
Antipasto Salad................................ 5.25
Linda's Fried Chicken Salad................................ 5.75
Mixed greens, with deep fried battered chicken strips, topped off with onions, black olives, red pepper rings, and tomato
Mary's Vineyard Salad................................ 5.75
Mixed greens, with fresh spinach, red onions, tomato, grilled chicken and bacon, served with honey mustard dressing
Kayla's Cobb Salad................................ 5.75
Mixed greens, with onions, green peppers, tomato, Swiss cheese, diced egg and bacon
Mitchell's Cordon Bleu Salad................................ 5.99
Mixed greens, tomato, red onions, topped with battered chicken strips, slices of ham and Swiss cheese

ON THE LITE SIDE - TRY ANY OF THESE SALADS:
TUNA
CHICKEN OR
EGG
In a tomato served on a bed of mixed greens

LINDA'S HONEY KORNER

Linda's Famous Flame Grilled or Deep Fried JUMBO Hot
Dog................................ 2.00
WITH FRIES AND SODA - $3.50
Koney Dog................................ 2.50
Flame grilled dog topped with Koney chili, diced onions and mustard
The ATOMIC Dog................................ 2.75
Flame grilled hot dog with chili, onions and jalapeno peppers
Loose Hamburger................................ 2.95
Ground beef seasoned to perfection, topped off with Koney chili and onions
Linda's Special................................ 3.25
Flame grilled hot dog smothered with Koney chili and ground beef topped off with diced onions and melted cheese

SANDWICHES / WRAPS

All sandwiches and wraps served with chips and a pickle spear.
ADD A CAN OF SODA FOR JUST $1.00 EA.

Chicken Greek Wrap................................ 4.75
Seasoned grilled chicken breast, lettuce, tomato, red onion, feta cheese topped with Greek dressing and rolled in a flat herb bread
Omelette Wrap................................ 4.75
Scrambled egg, bell pepper, onion, bacon, ham, American cheese, diced tomato, served on wheat flat bread with a side of salsa
Turkey Club Wrap................................ 4.75
Fresh sliced turkey breast, bacon, tomato, lettuce and mayo wrapped in herb flat bread
Chicken Salad................................ 4.75
Served on choice of bread, with lettuce and tomato
Egg Salad................................ 3.95
Made fresh to order, served on your choice of bread
Tuna Salad................................ 3.95
Made fresh to order, served on your choice of bread

FISH OUT OF WATER?

Mary's Fish & Chips................................ 6.99
Fresh fish, hand dipped in our own beer batter then deep fried golden brown
Deep Fried Shrimp Dinner................................ 6.99
Five jumbo hand-battered shrimp, fries, cole slaw and corn bread

47

BAKED SUBS

All subs are 8" - served with chips and a pickle spear.

House Special 6.25
Ham, salami, Italian sausage, fresh mushrooms, onions, bell pepper, mild pepper rings, cheese, lettuce, tomato, and house dressing

Chicken Sub 6.25
Seasoned grilled chicken, fresh mushrooms, onions, mild pepper rings, black olives, lettuce and tomato, topped with Greek dressing

Famous Philly 6.25
Finely sliced steak broiled with sautéed mushrooms, onions, bell pepper and melted Swiss cheese, topped with lettuce and tomato

Club Sub 6.25
Turkey, bacon, cheese, tomato, lettuce and mayo

Ham & Cheese 5.75

Veggie Special 5.75
Sautéed bell peppers, onions, fresh mushrooms and cheese topped with black olives, mild pepper rings, lettuce, tomato and house dressing

HOW ABOUT SOME BBQ?

Full Slab of Ribs 14.99
Slow cooked, flame grilled, and seasoned to perfection

Half Slab 7.99

Rib Dinner for Two 17.99
Full slab, fries, home-made slaw and breadsticks

Just for You 9.99
Half slab, fries, slaw and breadsticks

BBQ Chicken 6.99
Chicken deep fried chicken smothered in Mary's special BBQ sauce (6 pcs)

BBQ Chicken Dinner 8.99
Includes fries, slaw and breadsticks

MARY'S CLASSICS

Baked Mostaccioli 5.25
WITH GARDEN SALAD AND BREAD STICKS - $6.99

Cabbage Roll and Pierogi Dinner 6.99
Served with garden salad and corn bread

Chicken Parmesan 8.99
Seasoned chicken breast with marinara sauce, topped with melted mozzarella cheese, served with a side of spaghetti, garden salad and breadsticks

Linda's Homemade Lasagna 7.99
Served with salad and breadsticks

Tony's Spaghetti with meat sauce 5.75
WITH SALAD AND BREADSTICKS - $6.99

Beans and Cornbread 4.25
Slow cooked garlic beans served with cornbread and a side salad

FEEL LIKE CHICKEN?

Buttered Deep Fried Chicken Dinner 6.99
(leg, thigh, breast, wing) Served with fries, slaw and corn bread

Mary's Homemade Chicken Strips 5.99
A generous portion of sliced chicken breast strips seasoned and battered, then deep fried to golden brown, served with your choice of dipping sauce

Chicken Strip Dinner 6.99
Served with fries, slaw and corn bread

313-382-5555

MARY'S COMBO DINNERS

ALL DINNERS ARE SERVED WITH FRIES, COLE SLAW AND FRESH CORN BREAD

ONLY $12.99!!

#1 - RIBS & CHICKEN
(Half slab and 4 pieces of chicken)

#2 - RIBS & SHRIMP OR FISH
Half slab and 3 shrimp or 3 pieces of fish)

#3 - CHICKEN & SHRIMP OR FISH
(4 pieces of chicken and 3 shrimp or 3 pieces of fish)

#4 - SHRIMP & FISH
(3 shrimp and 4 pieces of fish)

MARY'S ULTIMATE COMBO

ONLY $26.99!!

SERVES 3-4 — GREAT VALUE!

RIBS – CHICKEN – SHRIMP – FISH

A half slab of ribs, 4 pieces chicken, 7 shrimp and 7 pieces of fish, served with fries, cole slaw and rolls!

BABYSITTER'S SPECIAL

TWO 16" PIZZAS
ONE W/CHEESE AND 1 TOPPING
ONE W/CHEESE AND 2 TOPPINGS
BREADSTICKS
& 2-LITER

ONLY $17.49

SUPER 24 SPECIAL

MONSTER 24" PIZZA
CHEESE AND 3 TOPPINGS
FAMILY SIZE GARDEN SALAD
BREADSTICKS

ONLY $24.24!

IT'S NOT FAST FOOD
IT'S HOMEMADE!

MARY'S KITCHEN

AT THE VERY LEAST YOU SHOULD USE A PAGE
OF YOUR BUSINESS FLYERS TO SCREAM OUT
YOUR ABILITY TO HANDLE LARGE ORDERS.
IDEALLY YOU'LL ALSO HAVE A SEPARATE
CATERING MENU (NEXT PAGES)

Mary's Kitchen

14729 Champaign Road
(Between Dix and Allen)
Allen Park MI 48101
MONDAY - THURSDAY 11 AM - 9 PM
FRIDAY & SATURDAY 11 AM - 10 PM
SUNDAY CLOSED
CATERING ANYTIME !

CARRYOUT
DELIVERY
CATERING

THE BEST PIZZA
BAKED SUBS
SANDWICHES & WRAPS
KIDNEYS & DEEP-FRIED HOT DOGS
BURGERS
FRIES & CHILI-CHEESE FRIES
CHILI AND BEEF STEW
FISH & CHIPS
PIEROGI
CABBAGE ROLLS
HOMEMADE SOUPS

LASAGNA
MOSTACIOLLI
STUFFED PEPPERS
BAKED MAC & CHEESE
PATTY MELTS
SHRIMP
HOT TURKEY SANDWICHES
COOKIES & DESSERTS
CHEESEBREAD
SALADS
WINGS

AND SO MUCH MORE!

Mary's Kitchen
Catering Menu
14729 Champaign Road
(Between Dix and Allen)
Allen Park MI 48101

FULL-SERVICE CATERING FOR:

BANQUETS
PARTIES
MEETINGS
WEDDINGS
BIRTHDAYS
REUNIONS
SPORTING EVENTS
FUND-RAISERS
PICNICS
HOLIDAYS
GRADUATIONS
BRIDAL SHOWERS
BABY SHOWERS
OPEN HOUSES
DROP-OFF, BUFFET OR TABLE SERVICE

All Events

313-382-5555
FAX 313-382-5511
maryskitchenallenpark@yahoo.com

Hello!

As busy as you are, it's difficult to plan a large gathering. Between choosing a menu, shopping, preparing, and serving, it's a full-time job, and *you already have one of those*. At MARY'S KITCHEN serving your food needs IS our full-time job, and we love it!

In addition to our regular menu, which has something for everyone and groups of every size, we've put together a CATERING MENU for special events. Whether it is a business meeting at the office, a family gathering, or a banquet for your sports team, with MARY'S KITCHEN you only have one task – decide which of the delicious items you want to have served, and we'll do the rest! From simple self-serve buffets to full-service, tell us what you want...we know what to do from there.

What could be tastier?

Mary

MARY'S KITCHEN
14729 CHAMPAION ROAD
ALLEN PARK MI 48101
313-382-5555
FAX 313-382-5511
maryskitchenallenpark@yahoo.com (for questions and comments)

Hot Dinners

Perfect for wedding receptions, banquets, reunions, luncheons, and many other events,.
Hot dinners could include:

CHICKEN
ROAST BEEF
MOSTACCIOLI
STUFFED CABBAGE
KEILBASA & SAURKRAUT
CORN
REAL MASHED POTATOES & GRAVY
GREEN BEANS
DINNER ROLLS
SALAD

Choose your style of service to meet your needs and budget

Drop-Off Buffet

We will prepare the meal and set it up for you. The pans and utensils are disposable, so when it is over you just throw them away!

Buffet with Servers

We'll have friendly servers on hand for your event to change empty pans, help serve your buffet guests, and do all the clean-up!

Table Service

Not only will we prepare a fantastic dinner, we'll serve it to your guests at their tables, bringing whatever they need for a fantastic experience.

The cost of HOT DINNERS depends on many factors, including number of people, the menu chosen, the style of service, and extras like beverages, desserts, or other specials needs. Let us know what you need, and leave the worrying to us!

Did someone say
BIRTHDAY

PARTY ?

LET MARY'S KITCHEN DO THE WORK

Birthday Parties
DELIVERED

JUST $6 PER PERSON

INCLUDES:

• 2 Slices - Cheese & 1 topping
• Soda
• Cake alteration
• Paper products
• Balloons

Goody Bag $2 extra per person

24-hour notice needed

**MARY'S
KITCHEN**
313-382-5555
FAX 313-382-5511

WARNING: WE TEND TO PAMPER OUR
CLIENTS. YOU ARE CAUTIONED TO
EXPECT INCREDIBLE SERVICE AND
EXCEPTIONAL FOOD, WHICH MAY
CAUSE HAPPINESS, ESPECIALLY IN
THE YOUNG OR OLD, MALE AND
FEMALE, AND ESPECIALLY ADULTS
AND CHILDREN.

Party Trays

	10-15 people	20-25 people
VEGGIE TRAY W/DIP Carrots, Broccoli, Cauliflower, Celery, and Bell Peppers	19.95	29.95
CHEESE & CRACKERS Cubed Cheeses, 3-4 varieties Crackers	15.95	25.95
FRUIT TRAY W/DIP 6 Fruits – variety of Pineapple, Watermelon, Cantaloupe, Kiwi, Strawberries, Red & Green Grapes, Honeydew, Starfruit	19.95	29.95
FRUIT & CHEESE 3 Fruits and 3 Cheeses	19.95	29.95
RELISH TRAY Variety of Pickles and Olives	9.95	19.95
DELI PLATTER 3 Meats, 2 Cheeses & 3 Breads Ham, Turkey, Salami, Roast Beef, Corned Beef Swiss, Cheddar, Provolone, Co-Jack, Jalapeno Wheat, White & Rye Breads	29.95	39.95
SANDWICH WRAP TRAY Chicken Salad, Tuna, Club, Egg Salad Original or Herb Wraps	19.95	
WING TRAY W/DIPPING SAUCES	29.95	39.95
SHRIMP RING W/ SAUCE	24.95	35.95

52

Salads

10-15 people		20-25 people
	HOMEMADE POTATO	
12.95		15.95
	BROCCOLI SALAD	
14.95		17.95
	COLE SLAW	
12.95		15.95
	ORIENTAL CHICKEN	
14.95		17.95
	ITALIAN PASTA	
12.95		15.95

Assorted Extras

APPETIZERS (COLD) - 2.75 PP

APPETIZERS (HOT) - 3.75 PP

Could include any 4 of the following:
- Miniature Meatballs in Sweet & Sour Sauce
- Bacon-Wrapped Scallops or Water Chestnuts
  - Stuffed Mushrooms
  - Chicken Drumettes
  - Mini Quiches
  - Mini Egg Rolls
  - Pizza Poppers
- Cocktail Sausages in Sauce

CHEESECAKE TRAY – 4.75 PP
DESSERTS (CLASSIC) – 3.00 PP
COOKIE TRAY – 1.50 PP

Fast & Easy Party Packages

#1 24/24 SPECIAL
- 1-24" Pizza w/ Cheese and 3 toppings
- Family-size Garden Salad
- Cheesebread
  $24.24

#2 GAME DAY SPECIAL
- 2 XL 18" Pizzas with Cheese and 3 toppings
- 2 Orders of Cheesebread
- Family-size Garden salad
- 40 Wings with Sauce
- 2 2-liters Soda
  $44.95

#3 PIZZA & PASTA SPECIAL
- XL 18" Pizzas with Cheese and 3 toppings
- Baked Mostaccioli
- Cheesebread
- Family-size Garden Salad
  10-15 people $48.00
  20-25 people $96.00

Party Subs

3-4-5-6 FOOT

EACH FOOT SERVES 2-4 PEOPLE
ONLY $8.95 PER FOOT

48 HOUR NOTICE NEEDED

THE BENEFITS OF BUSINESS WALKS:

- ❏ TREMENDOUS SOURCE OF CUSTOMERS
- ❏ $100 BUSINESS INCREASE GIVES $30 RESIDENT INCREASE
- ❏ REACH EVERY BUSINESS IN AREA
- ❏ CHANCE TO SELL REGULAR & CATERING ORDERS
- ❏ 5-15% RESPONSE RATE

COST: $48-96

RESULTS: $720-2160 IN TWO WEEKS. THIS METHOD WORKS YOU HARD, BUT GIVES YOU RESULTS!

STUDENT CUSTOMERS

Not all stores will have a large STUDENT CUSTOMER population. Certainly, if you're near a college campus you'll have plenty, but all stores have some. A STUDENT CUSTOMER is typically someone who:

- Is young, with an income through part-time job, full-time job, financial aid, or allowance;
- Alternates between periods of extreme cost consciousness (non-pay weeks) and reckless spending (pay weeks or financial aid checks);
- Late night eaters;
- Have only been in the community for a short time;
- Interacts with many other students.

This is where you violate the rule of not keeping both bicycles and Cadillacs on the same lot. These customers will be searching for low prices at times, for a LOT of food at other times, and for variety still other times. These are your your most schizophrenic of customers, but you can use that to great advantage by being what they need at the time. Far from confusing them (as it would with other types), they appreciate it. However, marketing to STUDENT CUSTOMERS is more than just picking the right combination of offers – remember, the competition could do the same thing (and if they see it working for you, they might try).

One of the best ways to market your store is to get your customers to market for you, and STUDENT CUSTOMERS are perfect for that. For example, if you are near a college dorm, advertise for *special agents*. You can "hire" one from each floor, give them t-shirts or other branding material (if it fits your budget) and give them special ad material. Their pay? Pizzas! Start them off with a free pizza every week. The ad material you give them will be coded, and they'll have good reason to get the material out for you, because for every $100 in orders you get from their coupons, they get another $5 in pizza – double that if the orders are delivered to their floor or their fraternity! You control the number of agents, and under-performers can be replaced by one of the many students who will be waiting in line to take the job!

No one can market for you better than your own customers, and no one wants pizza more than the STUDENT CUSTOMER.

TRANSIENT CUSTOMERS

Every store has a percentage of customers who are looking for the best price. Their loyalty is weak or non-existent; it could be based on low-income, on personal choice, or other reasons – the point is, typically you're not going to change their habits. Still, you wouldn't mind having them as customers, so every now and then......go fishing!

Fishing is seasonal, fishing is temporary (after a while it starts to stink); unless you have decided that price and value is going to be your USP, limit your fishing to specific days of the week, or just once a season, maybe once a year. Define the period, stick to it, make sure people know it's not normal. Then look at your menu and pricing: What can you sell, at a low enough price to beat the competitors, and still make money? Yes, you still need to make money on this. It's a promotion, but not a loss-leader. Most stores use a large pepperoni pizza, which is fine – it's a simple product with a decent profit margin. However, that's unimaginative, and there are some national chains really working hard to corner the market on that. If you can't beat them, or if you want to make a little more money, look at something else. Some possible examples are:

- "THE WORKS" PIZZAS – The extra toppings are mostly low-cost vegetables.
- COMBOS that include bread (cheap), salads (cheap), soft drinks (cheap) or other.....well, *cheap* items.
- Something FREE next week when you buy something now.

Will this work for you? You'll only know by trying. Some of your CURRENT CUSTOMERS will temporarily switch over to your fishing offer, so that might weaken sales in that area, but the increase in TRANSIENT CUSTOMERS, some of whom you'd hopefully keep after the offer has passed (because some weren't TRANSIENT at all, just NON-CUSTOMERS who needed an extra shove) will more than make up for it.

If you've done surveys and talked to your customers you have a lot of information, not only about your store but about your competitors. Sometimes the only way to increase your traffic of TRANSIENT CUSTOMERS is to directly attack your competitor by:

- ❑ Do what they do, only better;
- ❑ Do what they can't;
- ❑ If you can't do it better, make it look like you can.

It's often all in the packaging – for example, if the other guy can beat you on price hands down, then emphasize what he cannot do – delivery, high quality, bigger pizzas – there's always something you can beat him at.

OTHER METHODS THAT *WORK*

GOING SALE-ING – THE BEST MARKETING METHOD I'VE EVER USED

Until just recently, I thought this was my idea – that out of all the methods described in this book, this was the only idea which was completely and originally mine. I was proud of that. Imagine my disappointment when I was browsing through some 18-year-old files and found the first time I wrote down the method in any detail. It was pretty much the way I describe it here, except that at the bottom I had written "IDEA BY TOM PAWLAK." Tom was one of my bosses back then, and apparently he told me about it, I wrote it down, and a few years later used it, thinking it was my idea.

Thanks, Tom – and I apologize for all the times I took credit for it.

Throughout the summer garage sales, yard sales, tag sales, and all sorts of sales pop up in most areas. In the south they may even be year round. These are potential customers, and potential marketers.

The process is simple: You arrive at the sale the first morning, offering the family holding the event a free pizza in exchange for passing out flyers at their sale. I have done this for over 10 years, and have only been turned down twice. Usually they are thrilled to get a free pizza for something so simple. When I did this for the first time I went to about a half-dozen sales the first week; the second week, because it was successful I went to about a dozen; by the third week people were calling me to ask "Rich, I'm having a garage sale next week. How can I get your flyers?" One summer the pizzeria I worked with raised sales from $4300/week in June to over $6200/week in August, using ONLY this method! We started making sure we hit all the sales in our delivery area every week, missing no one. Later that summer some competitors tried to do it – *but no one would take their flyers*. We had become known as the "garage sale pizzeria" and had an unofficial exclusive franchise.

Some of your store sales will come from the people attending the garage sales. It was not unusual to get a phone call, "Yeah, I got three flyers of yours at three different garage sales; I guess I ought to try you." It was a terrific way to get the name and the menu into the hands of people who, for whatever reason, had never paid attention to us before. Even more important, though, were the people holding the sales. Yes, some would merely call to order their free pizza, and that was fine. Most, however, placed an order along with it, because one free pizza usually was not enough to feed the family. Some would order every day of the sale, because even though they only got one free pizza, they were using garage sale money ("free" money) and wanted to call the place that had given them a free pizza. These garage sale hosts became our most loyal customers, because no matter how many times they ordered, we were always the place that gave them a free pizza (see the section "WHAT ABOUT FREE?"). The first summer we used it, we visited over 200 garage sales, and most of those had been NON-CUSTOMERS. They became loyal customers, and gladly marketed for us.

My most successful
doorhanger ever. It was
hokey, it was a little
silly --- but it worked, and
maybe it worked because
it was hokey and silly.

THANK YOU
FOR PASSING OUT OUR FLYERS
AT YOUR SALE

FREE PIZZA

USE THIS CARD FOR A FREE
16" PIZZA WITH ONE TOPPING

The cost to do this is about 50 flyers per sale (very cheap, basic one-sided flyers like doorhangers), the cost of a pizza, and the time it takes each week to visit them. Using the local papers, you can map out a route, take a couple hours out of 2-3 days during the week, and let your new customers do the rest. If you hit 16 garage sales in a week, your cost should be:

FLYERS (800) - $8-16
FOOD COST FOR 16 PIZZAS - $40-48
TOTAL - $48-64

Your return will be at least $400 that first week on 16 sales. If you hit more sales, the results go up. The results get better in the second and third and consecutive weeks, because you not only get the exposure from the new sales, you have the loyalty of all those you served in previous weeks, and anyone who does a lot of garage saleing but hadn't responded to the first flyers will continue to be exposed to them.

It's a good idea to change flyers every week or so.

Recently I worked with a down-and-out pizzeria that was doing less than $100/day. Obviously there was no real marketing budget, so whatever I could suggest had to be very cheap, so I told them about this program. The owner used flyers I printed for her, she went to the sales herself, and a store that had never done more than $300 in any single day (even after sending out 5,000 *Mega-ads*), did $500 the first Friday, and doubled her sales in one week – ***doing only this***!

59

GARAGE SALE CERTIFICATE

THANK YOU

FOR PASSING OUT FLYERS AT YOUR GARAGE SALE, YOU CAN USE THIS LETTER FOR A FREE

MEDIUM PIZZA WITH 3 TOPPINGS

Yard Sale
Date
Place

ONLY FOR OUR GARAGE SALE FAMILIES

877 FIFTH STREET
OPEN 11AM-MIDNIGHT
DELIVERY $1.50

PIZZA SOCIETY

734-285-6971

GIFT CERTIFICATES

I can't think of anything better than getting money for a product you won't be making for a week or two. You get the food cost now, the labor cost now, and even the *profit* now. If someone buys a gift certificate as a gift, the person using it treats you as if *you* gave it to them as much as the purchaser did. Even if the original buyer uses it, they think of it as FREE food, and you get the loyalty benefits of that. You can offer a discount, because you get all your costs up front. Often certificates are shared and spread around, so your customers are marketing for you. They are slowly redeemed, which helps your bottom line. Over half the people order something more when they use a certificate, too. They are easy to print, easy to track, and easy to sell. Just look at the number of gift cards given over the last Christmas holiday - businesses love them, customers love them.

60

PIZZA CARD
This card is good for
one 16" PIZZA with
one topping at
MARY'S KITCHEN

Valid 12/26/06 through 2007
MARY'S
KITCHEN *(313) 382-5555*

"PROVE IT" CARDS

Every now and then you meet someone out in the world who has never heard of your store, or for one reason or another hasn't tried it. You're not walking around with menus in your pocket, but if you reach into your pocket and give them a "PROVE IT" card, chances are very good that you'll hear from them soon. They cost less than a penny each; business card sized, and can be a great long-term sales builder. Often these are given out during BUSINESS WALKS, too, which increases the response rate. The offer is usually something simple, a dollar off or a free bread item. As long as these aren't given out indiscriminately to CURRENT CUSTOMERS, they are a great tool.

BUSINESS-CARD SIZED "PROVE IT" CARD – FRONT AND BACK

FUND RAISER

There's nothing more valuable in the long run than getting involved in the community. Wherever you can find a place to do something for someone in town – especially if it will get you some publicity, you should do it. Make up a bunch of FREE PIZZA cards that the local football team can sell for a few dollars each. Make sure you get your food cost back, that the team makes money on each sale, and that the customer buying it gets a deal. You don't make money on the pizza, but you'll make money on the customer (see "WHAT ABOUT 'FREE'?" later in this book).

OTHER IDEAS WORTH EXPLORING:

- ♣ NEWSLETTER – Anything that keeps you in front of the customer's eyes longer.
- ♣ SAMPLERS – Find ways and reasons to get people to try your product.
- ♣ EMAIL MARKETING – Offer a daily or weekly special as an email-coupon.
- ♣ KID'S MEALS – There's reason why a certain burger chain has offered these for 30 years: because the kids decide where the family eats a large percentage of the time!
- ♣ BIRTHDAY PIZZAS – Give a man a FREE pizza on his birthday and he's often yours for the whole year.

There are other great ideas, but I don't want to write a book that would take a year to read. Want to hear more? Call me, write to me, or send me an email. Talk is always free.

WHY YOU NEED MULTIPLE MARKETING METHODS

WHY NOT PICK JUST ONE METHOD - THE ONE THAT SEEMS TO WORK BEST - AND JUST DO THAT?

If POSTCARDS get the best response, why not just send out more postcards and cut back on other things? If BUSINESS WALKS are the most successful method, why not save the printing and postage costs of other methods?

You might find a TV sitcom very funny, but a rerun – or worse, something rerun many times – can still get old. Ad agencies stop using successful commercials because they know that the viewer (or reader, or listener) needs to see something new or they will stop seeing it.

- ♣ DIFFERENT CUSTOMERS RESPOND TO DIFFERENT THINGS –AND YOU DON'T KNOW WHAT THE RIGHT PIECE IS UNTIL THEY CALL
- ♣ PEOPLE GET BORED WITH ADS THEY HAVE ALREADY SEEN
- ♣ 60% SAY NO FOUR TIMES BEFORE SAYING YES, BUT WITH TRADITIONAL MARKETING:

  - ❧ **44% ONLY HEAR FROM YOU ONCE**
  - ❧ **22% HEAR FROM YOU TWICE**
  - ❧ **14% HEAR FROM YOU THREE TIMES**
  - ❧ **12% HEAR FROM YOU FOUR TIMES**
  - ❧ **ONLY 8% GET 5-MORE EXPOSURES IN A YEAR**

SO, OUT OF 100 PEOPLE: 60% NEED FOUR OR MORE EXPOSURES, AND MOST BUSINESSES ARE ONLY HITTING 8% -- AND THEY MIGHT NOT EVEN BE THE RIGHT 8% !!

When you use multiple methods in a short span of time you have the best chance of getting the first-time customer.

63

When you show yourself in different ways, you have a better chance of finding what will attract that person.

THE COUPON KILLER

WE WILL ACCEPT
ANY VALID COUPON FROM
ANY PIZZA STORE - AND
OFFER YOU MORE!

That's right – we'll take any pizza store's valid coupon, and we'll
make it better!

VALID THROUGH 1-31-05
WHEN OUR PRODUCTS ARE DIFFERENT,
SEE STORE MANAGER FOR
ALTERNATIVE OFFER

GET THESE BONUSES, TOO!

- Collect (5) different pizza flyers from other pizza stores, and you
  can get a 12" cheesebread for just 99¢ with any order!
- Stop in and get some of our special "PROVE IT" cards, put your
  name on them, and give them to people you know. When five people
  order from us and use those $1-off cards, you get a free pizza!

KIDS AND STUDENTS:

- Bring in a report card with all A's and B's, and get a FREE 8"
  PERSONAL PIZZA!
- Bring in a picture of the FULL MONSTER enjoying BIG DADDY'S
  PIZZA, and get a free brownie – plus we'll put your picture on the
  wall!

**Big Daddy's
Pizza and Subs** and
Little Momma's
Ice Cream

HOME OF
THE FULL MONSTER
24" ROUND PIZZA

313-333-3333

SOMETIMES – *SOMETIMES* – GETTING REALLY AGGRESSIVE WITH YOUR COMPETITION IS A GOOD IDEA. THERE ARE TIMES WHEN YOU SHOULD NOT TRY TO COMPETE ON PRICE AT ALL. NOT SURE? EXPERIMENT ON A SMALL SCALE – OR LET'S TALK ABOUT IT!

THE TWO-WEEK PLAN

WEEK ONE SAMPLE SCHEDULE

MON	TUE	WED	THU	FRI	SAT	SUN
STEP UP CARDS				TWO TIMER CARDS		
BUSINESS WALKS						
		DOOR-TO-DOOR SURVEYS				
POSTCARD MAILING #1						
	LOST CUSTOMER LETTERS				DOORHANGING	
CURRENT CUST. SURVEY MAILING						

WEEK TWO SAMPLE SCHEDULE

MON	TUE	WED	TH	FRI	SAT	SUN
STEP UP CARDS				TWO TIMER CARDS		
BUSINESS WALKS						
		DOOR-TO-DOOR SURVEYS				
POSTCARD MAILING #2						
	NON-CUSTOMER SURVEYS					
					DOORHANGING	

The days will be full! Look at Wednesday of the Week One:

BUSINESS WALKS 9am-1pm
DOOR-TO-DOOR SURVEYS 3pm-7pm
MAILING OF POSTCARDS
MAILING OF SURVEYS
MAILING LOST CUSTOMER LETTERS

65

The weekend is not much easier – here's Week One Saturday:

DOORHANGING 8am-noon
DOOR-TO-DOOR SURVEYS 2pm-5pm

These are guidelines and approximations. You'll have to decide what schedule works best for your store, of course.

I can spout ideas all day long, but unless they're in a coherent plan that you can follow, it's no good. As I said in the beginning, this is not something you can just sit back and let happen – someone has to be working it. Whether that person is you, or someone you hire, someone has to be spending a lot of time. The effort doesn't just replace the money spent – that is, you're not just spending money on labor instead of more pieces to get the same result. The extra money and effort get a higher percentage of responses, and the loyalty of those new customers is much higher, because of the way they were attracted.

Again, there's a lot of work here, but we're not talking about some trivial matter --- this is the goal of raising your sales by $2,000/week and doing it fast. Of course it will take a lot of work, but the results are worth it.

I've tried to offer as much detail as I can while still taking into account the different personalities of each store. If there's anything you would like to hear more about, or any questions you have – call me!

RICH BUCHKO
906-369-0793

THE RESULTS

In two weeks THE TWO-WEEK PIZZA PLAN will reach at least 3220 potential NEW customers through one form or another (some will be contacted 2-3 times using the different methods) – which doesn't sound like a lot, but you will gain at least 192 NEW customers, all bringing you money. That's the difference between fishing and hunting. All the methods work separately & together, all the different types of customers are attracted for their own reasons – but they all come to you in two weeks. In the 3rd and 4th weeks the repeat sales and new customers (some will not have had time to respond in the first two weeks) will keep that increase in place, or take it higher!

TYPICAL RESULTS FOR THE TWO-WEEK PLAN

METHOD	PIECES (min.)	RATE	RESPONSE	SALES INCREASE
BUSINESS WALKS	1200	5-10%	60-120 x $12	$720-1440
NON-CUST. SURVEYS	220	15-30%	22-33 x $12	$396-792
CURRENT CUST. SURVEYS	(100)	N/A	N/A	N/A
POSTCARDS	600	10%	60 x $12	$720
LOST CUSTOMER LETTERS	200	10-15 %	20-30 x $12	$240-360
STEP-UP CARDS	(800+)	3-5%	???	???
TWO-TIMER CARDS	(600+)	3-5%	???	???
PROVE-IT CARDS	(1000+)	???	???	???
GARAGE SALES	???	???	???	???
DOORHANGING	1000	3-5%	30-50	$360-600
	3220		192-293	$2436-3912

Assuming the minimum responses, and completely ignoring those methods which either cannot be measured (garage sales, for example, vary too widely area-to-area) or cannot be quantified (anything going to a current customer, although it will cause many to order more often, or to order more, is not included), you'll see an increase of at least $2460 over the two-week period. If the response rate is higher, your return for each dollar spent will be greater.

I have to make assumptions as to costs in some cases, and results in others. Truth is, although most of these methods work for most stores in most cases, results do vary. I offer my word, though, that if you follow this plan, I guarantee results to your satisfaction or your money back.

A common question is: *If the results vary, and the costs vary, how and why do you guarantee a $5-10 increase for every dollar spent?*

Every pizzeria owner has to decide what return is satisfactory, how it compares to other methods, and whether it is worth the cost of this book. In short, it is an unconditional guarantee. If your return is $3 for every dollar spent, you might decide it wasn't worth doing. I don't know everything about pizza marketing, and I certainly don't know everything about your store and your people. I do believe in this program, and have proven it many times over – that's enough for me to guarantee you'll be happy.

AFTER TWO WEEKS

After two weeks you'll have a better picture of what works for your store, but I recommend these guidelines:

TWO TIMER CARDS – Do them for 3 weeks, then take two weeks off before resuming.

STEP UP CARDS – Keep on doing them!

POSTCARDS – What worked? What didn't? What would you like to try? Limited mailings to test products and prices and ideas are always good. Don't go widespread, though, until you know what will happen with an offer.

SURVEYS – Do at least 20 CURRENT CUSTOMER SURVEYS every week; do at least 100 NON-CUSTOMER SURVEYS every week.

LOST CUSTOMER– Any time someone has not ordered in 3 weeks, call or write.

BUSINESS WALKS – Visit every business at least every other month with something new.

DOORHANGERS – Do some every weekend.

The only hard and fast rule – *GET OUT AT LEAST 100 PIECES OF SOME KIND EVERY DAY*.

All the methods and ideas in this book have been tried and tested multiple times, and are here because most of the time, for most stores, they work well. No one method works every time for every store. Sometimes it fails. That's why we're not just doing one thing, because then failure is a horrible event. We're not spending hundreds or thousands of dollars on anything and ending up regretting it. We're trying, testing, using proven methods to see how they work in your store.

FAILURE DOES HAPPEN

And when it does, I hate it! One summer for The Seattle Pizza Company I convinced Jim, the owner, that we should have a special Father's Day promotion. I thought it was the perfect holiday – after all, dads love pizza, and people love their dad, right? We created new flyers, with special big offers, spent a couple hundred dollars on printing and distribution......and received one order from the flyers.

To this day I cannot explain why it was such a tremendous flop. Even our regular everyday flyers got a better response. It was such a horrendous failure that for two years whenever I would make a suggestion Jim was unsure about he would smile and say, "Just like Father's Day, eh, Rich?"

If I sound like a broken record when I tell you how important it is that you try things on a small scale and see how they work before investing a lot of money into the idea, this is why.

Not everything works. I am hoping one day to get a letter from a pizzeria owner telling me about his successful Father's Day promotion – I'd like to know how to make it work.

HIRING A CRS

One thing about the strategies in this book – they require some time and effort. You might be willing to put forth the effort (you ought to be willing – it's your store), but you still may not have the time. Consider hiring a CRS – *Customer Relations Specialist*. The primary functions of a CRS are to:

♣ Schedule and handle the distribution of all marketing.
♣ Make customer callbacks, and be the first point of contact when any customer calls.
♣ Handle the data entry for customer information (or keep the customer books if you aren't using a computer)
♣ Handle all promotions, store decorations, or other customer-contact items

This person could be an existing employee who has shown terrific customer relations skills, or it could be someone you hire specifically for the job. Depending on the responsibilities you give to him or her, it could take 15-20 hours out of the work week, so its possible that you could expand a part-timer's position.

The CRS is not just someone to run around for you. That person will be in contact with the customers as much as you are, maybe even more, so he or she has to be as good as you at handling people – even better, if that is possible. Superior phone voice, pleasant attitude, a willingness to listen and ability to show genuine concern are essential traits. Although the CRS can be male or female, from here on we will use "she" and "her" when talking about the CRS – but that does not mean that a man cannot be a great CRS.

Here are just some of the responsibilities that a CRS will take care of:

1. Do a minimum of 10 customer callbacks every day, and keep a record of the information. This means actually talking to customers, not getting 5 *no-answers* and counting those in the mix.

2. Make sure that at least 100 pieces of advertising get out every day. If you have 5,000 inserts hitting on Wednesday, you still need to get 100 pieces out on Thursday – preferably somewhere that was not covered by the Wednesday advertising.

3. Monitor the supply of advertising material in the store, to be sure that you do not run low. The CRS will also keep track of expiration dates. We aren't going to be concerned about most expiration dates, but we don't want to be putting out material that the customer will perceive as old or no longer any good. If the customer doesn't THINK you will accept it, its worthless.

4. Track coupons received to evaluate what is working and what isn't. Again, we aren't going to worry about whether or not the customer forgot to give us the coupon – that kind of pickiness doesn't build sales. But we still want to have an idea, in the broad sense, of what is working for us. If we get 125 coupon #1's back and only 3 coupon #2's, that tells us a lot!

5. Keep a customer order file. If you have a computer system that does most of that for you, great. But many pizza stores don't – and most don't need them to be successful in tracking the customer orders. Any information you have about what the customer orders is useful. This will occupy a lot of the CRS's time, particularly if you don't use a computer program, but is essential to building sales over the long haul.

6. Handle most customer complaints. The CRS will have to be trained on how to do this, and will have to be taught how to

71

know when it is time to turn a problem over to the manager, but you want your CRS to do this whenever possible. It's not that you are ducking the customer – in fact, once the problem is resolved you will want to make contact with the customer, introduce yourself and see that everyone is happy. But your CRS has been designated as the know-all see-all of your customers, and so she should be the person handling most small matters – and we want all complaints to be small matters.

7. Hire, supervise, and evaluate all doorhangers.
8. Keep the store in good image, particularly in regards to the outside of the store. This does not mean that your CRS will do all the cleaning, any more than it means she will be doing all your advertising. It just means that she will know what the situation is, and what needs to be done, and when necessary, find the person to do it.
9. Keep employee records, and take care of periodic MVR checks. This doesn't fall under the heading of customer relations, specifically, but takes just a few minutes each week and relieves you of one more responsibility.

This is just a partial list of what a CRS can do for you. You can concentrate on the store operations, food quality, cost control, and immediate customer satisfaction. He or she could be an assistant manager who uses part of the week for these responsibilities, but he or she HAS TO BE ABLE TO SPEND TIME FOCUSING ON JUST THESE ITEMS, not just try to work them into the day. If you think that will become a problem, hire someone just to be your CRS – you won't regret it.

SALES SLUGGISH? RAISE YOUR PRICES!

It sounds like a crazy idea, and for most of us it is, but every now and then there's a problem with your pizza that you couldn't see – the price is too low. As we've already covered, some people are looking for Cadillacs, won't even consider a bicycle, and their yardstick for determining the two is price.

Again, I'm not suggesting it for most people – in fact, for most of us it would be a bad idea – but if you've truly worked hard at your marketing, have a good product, get good reviews and are wondering what the heck is going on, maybe you're underselling yourself.

James Earle had been operating his store for two year, had made some money, but had never seen the sales grow. We worked on his marketing, and we did everything we could think of, and more. Sales increased, but there was something in the back of our minds that told us this wasn't the ceiling. A very large percentage of his customer base was tourist/visitor trade – probably 60% or more most weeks. This meant he couldn't build long-term relationships with a lot of his potential customers. He thought the key was to have the best price in town, so during their stay (usually 1-2 weeks) they'd have reason to visit. That makes sense, of course – people on vacation want a good value, too, right?

But what's value? They can get a $10 pizza at home. Maybe this week they want something more special.

Overnight we jacked up the prices 100%, and crossed our fingers.

Sales increased – not just the revenue, but the customer count!   The actual sales increase was over 140% and the customer count increased by 20%.   How did that happen? People who came to town on vacation, as I said, could get a "normal" pizza at home but they were looking for a treat, something special, something out of the ordinary.

It's true that Jame's residential customers were a little shocked by the price increase, but since James continued his

73

normal coupon price to those customers they not only didn't mind, they were ecstatic – you see, now the locals were getting a better deal than the tourists. The tourists had their Cadillacs; the locals had a great deal and a sense of community pride; James had a windfall in his profits.

It's a rare store that will be right for this kind of tactic, but it does happen. Like I said, there's plenty of room in the world for Cadillac dealers and bicycle dealers – just determine which one your customers want, and give it to them.

OR ... EXTREME PRICE RAISING

A pizza-chain franchisee shared his technique for maximizing profit. Once his store had been open for a while, he would raise the prices by $1 across the board and see what happened. If the extra money he made was more than the number of customers he lost, he considered it a success, and would up the price another $1 to see what happened. He knew he would lose customers, but decided that he would look for the optimum sales-per-customer approach. For example,he might have 1,000 customer that spent $12 each, or $12,000/week. If he raised the price by $1, and the next few weeks he had 950 customers x $13 = $12,350, he was making more money on less work/people. If he raised it another $1 and the customer count went down to 900 X $14 = $12,600, even better, he thought. At 850 x $15 = $12,750 his increase was only slight, so he would stop rather than risk dipping down. From his perspective he was making an extra $750/week while serving 150 fewer customers, and since this was all added to the bottom line, he was indeed maximizing his profit-per-customer.

I still don't know what I think of this. On the one hand, he's definitely finding out what his customer base is willing to pay and making the most of it; on the other hand, it's very a risky way to figure that out and the loss of 150 customers over the course of time scares me. Didn't I say earlier that each lost customer could cost you $1,758? $263,700 is a lot of money, even if you have to work a little harder for it.

I'm still studying this. I share it because I do believe that sometimes you want to be a Cadillac, and I do believe that sometimes raising your price is the right thing to do – but the scale of this still makes my head shake.

On the same note, my first book *The Two Week Pizza Plan*, first published in 2008, sold for $9.99. I felt that was a good price, it gave me some profit, and people liked the value. The time came last year when costs increased a bit, and raising the price became worth consideration. I was concerned that a jump might impact sales significantly – and they did. I have sold many more at $12.99 than at $9.99.

People will surprise you, every time.

Thankfully.

WHAT ABOUT "FREE"?

Okay, right on the heels of talking about raising prices I talk about giving away pizzas. You're certainly not going to do both at the same time – maybe neither one is right for you – but it's another option to explore.

If you gathered a large group of pizza storeowners/operators into any room and threw out the question, you'd get a wide range of responses: To some, the concept of giving product away FREE is a terrific marketing tool; to others, it is a great ad-word, as long as it is couched in the right combination of fine print and exceptions; still others would say that nothing should go out the door unless you make at least some money on it.

To accept the value of FREE, you have to accept that the pizza business is a long-term relationship. If everyone in your town came to visit your store only once, or only on rare occasions, you would fold before long. You need repeat, regular customers – and sometimes you have to lure them away from wherever they are currently a repeat, regular customer. We'll take it as a given that you have a smooth operation, and are capable of keeping customers once you get them in the door, but you still have to get them in. You can't just rely on random chance, and often you can't rely on your current marketing methods (even my terrific ideas) to make the difference.

But FREE?

Yes, FREE – and not FREE when you do this or that, FREE only on certain days or with certain conditions, but downright, simply FREE.

AND make money at it!

Why? There are a few reasons, including that you have a good product which, if tried by new customers, will result in sales on the merits of the quality. There's also, however, the human tendency to feel obligated to someone who has given us a gift, done us a favor, been unexpectedly nice to us. We are often not even aware of the Rule of Reciprocity, as coined by Robert Caldini in his excellent book *Influence*.[1] Why do many charities include small gifts of address labels or greeting cards with their donation requests? Because more people send money back after they receive a gift; they feel a sense of obligation. Many people don't like to be beholden to others, and the urge to reciprocate is strong even when it is not a conscious trait. As Caldini points out, waitresses receive larger tips when they leave a mint with your bill, Hare Krishnas receive more donations when they give a flower at the airport, and we make a point of sending Christmas cards to those who have sent them to us in the past.

Don't worry that your customers will dislike you for your cunning. Some might be aware that part of your intention is to get them to feel obligated to order something and spend money, but most won't get that far in their thinking – to most people, you're giving it away and they are happy to receive it. To most people the rule of reciprocity will not even register, or if it does they will dismiss it as unimportant. Those few who do understand that you're not only trying to showcase the quality of your product but also trying to induce a sense of obligation, are those who use it themselves and therefore won't be offended. In most cases, though, they'll still feel that obligation, or the familiarity of a kindred spirit, and will respond favorably.

For most pizza stores the common FREE product is a simple pepperoni pizza, or something your store offers that no one else can. If the food cost is reasonably low ($3-4), it will work, and the more you give away, the more money you make. Here's one example:

---

[1] Caldini, R. (2001). *Influence: Science and Practice.* Boston: Allyn and Bacon.

Make up 200 FREE cards – for this example we'll say it is a small pepperoni pizza with a basic food cost of $4. Hand them out – to people on the street, to businesses, to the teller at the bank, whomever it may be that **has not tried** your pizza before. Don't give out too many in one place; spread them around the neighborhood. Again, this is a card for a FREE PIZZA – no conditions, no restrictions.

The redemption rate varies widely, but let's say that out of the 200 distributed, 100 come back; the typical results would be higher, but let's be conservative. Of those 100 new customers, 60% or more will order a normal ticket average with their FREE pizza! They are part of a group, part of a family, or just plain hungry, so a great percentage have the add-on sales --- and now you have:

100 X 60% = 60 orders X $12 (ticket average) = $720 sales increase

What did it cost you to increase your sales by $720?

100 X $4 = $400

If I told you that you would be able to increase your sales by $720, get 100 *NEW* customers to try your product, and that you wouldn't spend the $400 unless you actually had the sales, would you say "Yes"? Think about the last marketing promotion you tried. Did you have the guarantee that it would only cost you if the cards were redeemed? No. More likely if you spent $400 you were hoping for an increase that would cover that cost. If your food costs are 33%, then you would need $532 just to cover the marketing and food, not to mention the labor and other expenses. Do you get $532 in NEW business when you spend $400, or do you get a lot of current customers taking advantage of your discounts, just spending less money than they normally would?

I am intentionally using high cost figures and low ticket averages, because I want to show that even under the worst of conditions, it can still be a good idea.

77

That's the best part of this process --- Other than the small cost of printing the cards and the time it takes to distribute them, you have NO extra advertising costs, the extra food cost only comes into play if the cards are redeemed, and most will buy more product! The more you hand out, the greater your sales increase.

EVERY FREE PIZZA CARD REDEEMED WILL RESULT IN AN INCREASE OF AT LEAST $7 WITHIN 10 DAYS.

Would you spend $4 to be *assured* of a $7.00 increase in sales from a NEW customer? I think most would.

Of course, there are those who say "Wait, if I'm spending an extra $4 on top of my regular food cost, I sure won't make much on that extra $7.00." Good point – except we're not just after their money today, we want it all the time. Yes, we want to buy our dimes for a nickel and sell our nickels for a dime, but this is a long-term relationship. And we're not giving out pizzas to everyone, we're not giving out thousands, we're sampling the area to people who have never tried you before. Let's look at our conservative example again:

> 200 Distributed / 100 Returned
> Cost to make 100 Pizzas = $400
> 60% Order with FREE pizza X $12 average = $720

You've given away 100 small pizzas to 100 new customers. If you only get ½ of them to come back a second time (this time with no FREE pizzas), you'll add another $600 to your sales. If only ¼ come back a third time, that's still another $300. So the $400 marketing cost has become $1620 in sales – and that's if you're doing a very bad job of customer retention! If you do a good job and can keep many of those customers for a year (2X a month X 12 months X $12 = $288 each), your sales increase reaches into the thousands – Over $14,000 if you only keep ½ of them that long.

Of course, there is a *wrong* way to do this:

♣ Choosing a high food-cost or labor intensive item;
♣ Giving them to current customers;

♣ Handing them to people that aren't likely to be customers;

♣ Distributing them to kids/teenagers, who are less likely to add-on to their order;

♣ Doing too many at once.

Pizza is a long-term relationship - a FREE pizza is a great way to make that first impression. If you can handle the sales, if you have a system in place for tracking and retaining your customers, every card you give away brings you $3.50 in sales within 10 days, every one redeemed brings $7.00 within 10 days – over the course of a year, each one handed out means $43 and each one redeemed is $86. Hand out 100, make $4300 more this year; hand out 1000 (over time) ......

FREE is a very good idea, if done right.

SIMPLIFY SIMPLIFY SIMPLIFY

Typically, if you can make money at it, it doesn't stop you from making money somewhere else, and people like it, I would say better to have it than not. Sure, frozen deep-fried artichoke hearts have a 48% food cost, but the little old ladies down the road like it and they spend $600/year, so what does it hurt? I believe, generally, in diversification of product --- but I also believe in simplification of operations, and there are times when you should do just the opposite of trying to have whatever the customer needs.

Marc's Pizza was a shop in a suburb of a large city. The clientele was middle class and business. He bought the store form a guy who had owned it a few years, and he had bought it from a buy who had owned it a few years, who bought it from a guy who had owned it a few years.... but no one seemed to notice a pattern. It each case, the new owners bought what appeared to be a thriving business with tremendous potential, struggled along for a while, tried new ideas, new products, a new name, and new marketing, then after a few years sold it to the next guy for a little less than he paid. I know from research that this same pizzeria had gone through 5 owners in twelve years.

Marc called me because he, too, had enough and wanted to sell, but he didn't want to sell for a big loss, and he didn't want to – as most likely others had done before him – lie about sales to inflate the selling price (and yes – it is amazing how many people simply take the word of the previous owner regarding average sales). He was hoping that I would come in, work my two-week pizza plan, bring sales to a level that could impress a new buyer, and get away with only a small loss. It was a sound, if only slightly devious, idea.

When I reached the store for the first time, I confess that I was confused. The product was good. The neighborhood held a lot of promise. The marketing seemed decent. I could understand why a new pizza owner would believe, at first glance, this is a good place and think *I'll bet I could make it work, even if the other guy couldn't.*

Three days later my mind had been completely changed and the problem was obvious. I sat down with Marc.

"You can't make money in this store the way things are – it cannot be done."

Admittedly, I could have started better, but I have a flair for the dramatic and I wanted to make sure he didn't misunderstand. Over the course of the next hour I explained why he couldn't make money. The store was very small – so small, in fact, that he couldn't keep more than a couple days worth of food on hand, either in the walk-in (a word that barely even applied there) or the freezer (which is probably larger in your home). As a result he was getting food at higher prices. Now, this he knew, but truth to tell, that was a minor problem compared to the ovens, which were simply too small to hold all the product he offered. He had two 3/4-sized deck ovens, used the top for pizzas and the bottom for non-pizza items, including ribs, wings, and a host of other products that typically I would love to see offered. When he got the calls he needed in order to be profitable, he didn't have room. Service time suffered because a pizza might be ordered 20 minutes before there was room for it. His single deep fryer couldn't handle much, either. The size of the store made profit impossible.

With his product mix, the resulting food cost, and over space, it was simply impossible for him to ever do more than $150/hour. Can you imagine being a resident of that neighborhood, trying pizza place after pizza place in the same location, and always finding that the service times were slow – year after year, owner after owner? It's little wonder that people had given up.

Marc explained that he couldn't just close the doors – he had too much invested in this place, and he needed to find a way to make it work.

"Then you have to use your ovens only for pizza," I told him. If his ovens were full of pizza instead of other products, he could do a higher volume, have a lower food cost, and actually make money while delivering decent service times.

"What about all the other products?"

I'll be honest – when we sat down I didn't know what the answer was. I was still trying to understand the problem. But when he asked me that question the entire solution just appeared in my head. Either my mind had never worked at so fast a pace before, or there was magic in the air. I started talking and didn't stop for a half hour. It began with:

"Get rid of them – all of them."

The idea was revolutionary, but simple. I told Marc that the only way he could make money was to dump every product that required a lot of storage space and required a higher food cost. He should make only pizza or pizza-related products. Really, it's not so revolutionary because in my chain days of the late '80's/early '90's we only sold pizza - - but here it seemed like a radical concept. By getting rid of everything that was frozen or prepared (what they like to market as 'value-added' when it is really only cost-added) his freezer space would be sufficient to store his pizza products, thus making it possible to get better pricing. His walk-in space would improve. Most importantly, his ovens would carry only pizzas, which are the best profit producers, and the core of the business. No fries, no burgers, no wings, no mozzarella sticks, no subs or salads, no ribs or BBQ anything – simply pizza. The name of the store? *Simply Pizza.*

If it couldn't be made with pizza dough and the ingredients that are used for pizza, he shouldn't sell it. In the end along with a selection of soft drinks there were three products: pizza, breadsticks, and something to throw in the deep fryer which you can learn about on page 85. That's it.

In many ways it flew in the face of everything I had learned and everything I had been teaching – to expand the menu, give people more reason to buy from you, give them more options to increase the ticket average, and all sorts of other conventional, logical, and time-honored reasons. The problem with the conventional wisdom, however, is that for twelve years it just wasn't working in the store, and even if someone could find ways to tweak it into profitability, the customers had tired of trying, and the store would never be able to do a volume that would make it worthwhile in the long run. It wasn't an easy idea to sell, but Marc and I shared one very important trait in common – we were both good at reaching a decision when it was obvious we had no choice.

One good thing about simplifying as compared to expanding: it's less costly. Within a few days all we had in the store were the pizza products, and the beginnings of a marketing campaign. The first few weeks were slow. I know there were days when Marc wondered if he had made the wrong choice, and there was a time or two when I wasn't feeling so confident, either. Slowly over the course of a month, however, people started coming in. The curiosity factor got them, and the idea got them.

One of the ways we emphasized the simplicity of the concept was the pricing. Nothing was $4.99 or 12.99 – everything was in whole dollars. Pizzas prices didn't change when you bought two; the cost of a pizza was the cost of a pizza. There weren't ten different prices for a large pizza because the store had ten different toppings; there were three tiers of pricing:

LARGE PIZZA
1-2 TOPPINGS - $6
3-5 TOPPINGS - $7
6-10 TOPPINGS - $8

And prices were all tax-included, so when someone ordered a $7 pizza, they paid $7, period. It meant an extremely simplified menu, a lot simpler bookkeeping, and once customers got used to the idea, they were pretty happy about it. They acted like they were getting it tax-free, when in fact the tax was included in the price.

There were people who wanted products Marc didn't have, and there were some lost sales because of it – but given the history that was an unavoidable price of doing business. Pizza, breadsticks, and the simplified menu kept costs low, easier to control, and suddenly there was room – both in the store to move around, and in the oven. In six weeks *Simply Pizza* was making money, and for the next two years was very successful. Marc got married, had a baby, and decided it was time to move on. When he sold the store, new owner decided it would be a good idea to have a more traditional expanded menu, go back to the ..99-pricing system, charge tax separately, and make things more like the way the "big guys" do it. Last I heard he was thinking of selling because the business wasn't doing very well.

And the cycle continues......

This story is not designed to get anyone to change the way they do business overnight. It's not a "look how smart I am" story (although I am pretty proud of it and I love to tell the story). It's here because sometimes we forget that the obvious answers are completely different from the traditional answers. Just as there are Cadillac dealers and bicycle dealers, there are pizzerias which are designed to be shopping malls and those which are designed to be boutiques, When you try to make one out of the other, it never works.

NEGOTIATE THE SALE

It's an accepted fact that people want to feel good about where they buy their pizza. They want to believe it is a good product, that the people are decent, and that they got a good value. But what really makes someone happy about a deal? When they think they got it for themselves, and maybe – just maybe – not everybody did. This is one of the reasons coupons

83

are so popular: because they suggest a special value that the person will not get without having that piece of paper. It doesn't matter that everyone gets the coupon price; what matters is how it feels. Well, if you can take it a step further and make the customer believe he made his own deal, not that you "gave" it to him but instead that he "got it" from you, you have a customer who's extremely happy.

Let's say you have a large pizza that you typically offer at a coupon price of $10.99, even tough on your menu the price is $14.99. You have a lot of leeway here, especially since you're still making money, most likely, at $9.99.

You'll want to make sure this special deal isn't going to current customers, but only to people that you know do not order from you. Send them your menu, without coupons (which you should always have – a regular price menu). Along with it send a letter introducing yourself and telling this customer that you'd like him(her) to try your pizza, and if he's not happy with your prices, you're going to make him a special deal – he can call you and make you an offer! That's right, invite the customer to haggle with you! Does this sound crazy? Only a little, and not every customer will like this idea, but for some people the chance to make a deal that no one else can get is just too tempting. Your top price is on the table, and you're giving him the chance to talk you down.

Beforehand you'll decide what the lowest discount you're willing to accept, because of course you still want to make money. Maybe you'll decide that 40% is your lowest discount. Keep in mind that your coupon price is about a 25% discount, so you're not dropping much farther than that. In any case, you're ready for the call. When he calls, ask him how much of a discount he wants. If he gives you a dollar amount, convert it to a percentage and try to keep him talking in percentages – its more impressive. If he says something silly like 50% off, you make a counter offer of 20% and give him a chance to respond. If he gives you something reasonable – say 30% – you give it some thought and say, "Okay, you've got a deal!" You'll tell him that you can't haggle all the time, but you wanted to get him to try your pizza and it's worth making a special deal, even if he did get you for a hefty discount. Maybe he did. Maybe he didn't, but he'll feel like he did.

Obviously, this is not a mass-marketing campaign, because negotiating with customers takes time, and you're not trying to become an appliance store – you're taking special steps to attract those customers who have not been paying attention to your regular marketing.

The feeling of having made a good deal is strong and long lasting. Being given a good deal is fine; getting one through effort, something to be proud of, is even better and is going to make your pizza taste that much better.

BUSINESS-CARD SIZED FREE PIZZA CARD
FRONT AND BACK

THE HOLIDAYS AND SPECIAL EVENTS CAN SNEAK UP ON US QUICKLY – TRY TO THINK TWO MONTHS AHEAD AT LEAST, AND BE A CAPITALIST. TAKING ADVANTAGE OF SEASONS, HOLIDAYS AND EVENTS IS NOT CRASS AND COMMERCIAL – IT'S JUST GOOD BUSINESS, AND IT'S WHAT PEOPLE WANT.

85

BOXTOPPING / BOUNCE BACK COUPONS

Want to waste a lot of money? Boxtop your coupons indiscriminately. If the customer orders two pizzas, make sure that exactly the same coupon is attached to each. Do it automatically, the same way every time.

Look, I don't mind spending money to attract potential business – if you've read any of this book you already know that -- but I hate to waste it, and most box-topping is totally wasted money.

Does that mean that you shouidn't send a coupon to your customer? I didn't say that; I've already talked about TWO-TIMER CARDS and STEP-UP CARDS. Most box-topping consists of gluing or stapling whatever flyer you have the most of on every pizza box (or every other pizza box). That kind of get-it-all-out-there approach works fine when you are trying to attract new customers with very cheap pieces, and you don't know who is going to be enticed by what kind of ad piece. But here you have an existing customer, someone for whom you already know the order history, maybe even their patterns. You know what they want, and what they don't. It's time to be a little more creative.

BOXTOPPING RULES:

1. DON'T attach the coupons to the box. In the world of pizza, how long after the pizza is gone does the box last? Not terribly long, and most of the time the coupon – even if it is a good one – is forgotten and ends up with the trash at the curbside. The coupon offer or flyer should accompany the pizza order, either slipped between the boxes or stuck in the seam of the box for easy removal - or better yet, hand it to your customer.

2. DON'T send a generic coupon when you already know what the customer has ordered. A menu? - Sure, if you think the

86

customer might not know all you have to offer, but why would you send a coupon for two medium pizzas to someone who just ordered two large pizzas? Why would you send the coupon for the $5 Monday special to someone who is already ordering $15 worth of pizzas on Sunday night? Use STEP UP CARDS and TWO-TIMER CARDS.

3. You aren't going to do all your marketing here. Your biggest marketing tool here is your quality pizza and your fast, friendly service. If you have these you have already gone a long way toward keeping that customer. If you don't, no amount of couponing can help you.

4. DO make sure you send a coupon and/or menu to everyone. If you don't like the idea of sending specific coupons to specific customers, then at least make sure they all get something.

SECTOR ANALYSIS

This fancy-sounding name is a simple way to find out where your strongest and weakest concentrations of customers reside – I just like the way the name sounds. This assumes you have address records – if you don't, then you should start right away. Even get your carry-out customers to provide their address – as you've seen, there are many uses for it!

Take a map of your delivery area, and divide it into sections no more than ¼ mile long or wide. Often there will be natural boundaries (rivers, hills) or man-made boundaries (freeways, major intersections) that will guide you. Number the sectors; then take your customer addresses and start marking the map, tracking how many of your customers come from each sector. It wouldn't be surprising to find that your greatest concentration of customers is closer to your store, and that the farther away you get, the fewer the customers. You might find the unexpected, though – the reasonably close sector with fewer sales than average. Why? Are one of your chief competitors located in that sector? Is there a boundary between you and the customer that creates in their mind the appearance you are too far away? Maybe this sector just doesn't get the same marketing material as the rest of your area, or perhaps the population in that area is very small. Whatever the reason – and it's not always easy to know what that reason is – combat it.

1. Track it on a weekly basis, locating the weakest 2-3 areas.
2. During that week, concentrate your marketing on those areas – postcards, doorhanging, surveys, etc. – this won't be the only area, but it will get more time.
3. At the end of the week those areas should no longer be your weakest. Someplace else will - now you'll have new candidates to focus your efforts during the following week.

If you concentrate your marketing on your weakest areas, and continually improve them, you'll quickly reach a point where you have no weak areas!

ANOTHER AGGRESSIVE CARD – DEFINITELY NOT FOR EVERYONE. HOWEVER, RATHER THAN DISCOUNT YOUR PIZZA PRICE FOR A SPECIAL "FAMILY MEAL," THINK ABOUT KEEPING THE PIZZA PRICE THE SAME AND OFFERING ADD-ONS FREE. IN THE END YOUR PRICE IS THE SAME, BUT THAT WORD "FREE" IN SOME AREAS WORKS MAGIC WHERE DOLLARS OFF WOULDN'T GET A SECOND LOOK. THE COST OF THE BREAD, SALAD AND SODA MIGHT EVEN BE LESS THAN WHAT YOU PLANNED TO DISCOUNT THE PACKAGE.

THE STORY OF STEVE

People buy for the reasons covered earlier, but they don't see it that way. They don't realize that at the end of the day they want to feel good about their choices. To the customer, it's either your fault, or to your credit. Encouraging someone to buy from you involves not only providing something the competition cannot, but making the customer like you. From time to time you have opportunities with each regular customer – moments when you can help the relationship or hurt it. Surveys, conversation, quiet mufflers, clean stores, and many other factors go into the overall picture, and it is not always what you think it is.

What is your goal? You want the customer to believe he or she is at the right place. When you have built loyalty you insulate yourself from price wars, protect yourself from snap subjective judgments, and ensure that any complaint is brought to you calmly and with respect. You made the customer like you, and now your customer will make sure you have the chance to keep it that way.

Some time ago, I was the manager of a medium-volume pizza store in a small Midwestern suburb for a large carry-out pizza chain. We had a good Friday dinner, and during the peak hours would have 10-15 people waiting in the lobby at any one time. In the lobby we also had a large full-color poster, depicting one of the pizza slices being lifted from the rest of the pie. In the picture, as the slice is lifted the cheese strings down, still attached to the rest of the pie, as if the cheese refused to release. It was a terrific picture, but one I came to hate because of Steve.

Steve (yes, his real name, there's no need to protect him) came in to order pizza that one Friday, but when he received it, he opened it in the lobby, lifted a slice, and started to complain - loudly, rudely, and colorfully. He was unhappy, it seemed, because his cheese separated when he lifted the slice – that is, it didn't string down and try to stay attached to the rest of the pizza. I apologized, explained that the pizza was very hot, I'm sure it would be very tasty, but for whatever reason, he wanted the pizza to "look like the one on your wall." I offered to make him another, which he readily accepted, and I created a pizza with a significant amount of extra cheese. I watched the pizza bake, and even took it to the front counter to cut the pizza in front of Steve, but despite all my efforts, when he lifted the slice it did not act like the picture. Not merely disappointed, but angry, Steve yelled and screamed and made all manner of anatomically-impossible suggestions. I had no clue how to handle Steve – especially since this was my first stint as a store manager. Eventually he left, but not immediately, and not without causing my other customers a great deal of discomfort.

Steve's last comment was that he would return, and I remembered that McArthur-like pronouncement the following week when I called the marketing department to see why their pizza acted differently than mine. I learned that the pizza was normal in all respects, except that the slice which was lifted did not contain the usual ground blend of two different cheeses, but instead was made with a solid slab of straight mozzarella cheese. The pure mozzarella, I was told, was much less likely to separate. I filed the information in my head, hoping never to need it.

Of course, Steve wasn't going to leave me alone. The following Friday he arrived, smack in the middle of the main dinner rush, demanding that I make him a pizza like that in the photo. By this time I hated Steve, and I wasn't too thrilled with whomever had taken that picture, either; but I told Steve to have a seat and I would take care of it for him. A little more than 10 minutes later I came to the counter with a pizza, carefully sliced it, and taking great pains to make sure I lifted the one slice I had made with the pure mozzarella, I lifted. It was beautiful! The cheese refused to release, and as I rose the slice higher, the cheese was stringing down – just like the picture!

Steve was beside himself. He jumped and shouted with joy, grabbed my hand to introduce himself, and sang my praises. He told me how terrific I was, and that he wanted me to make all his pizzas. For a while I wasn't sure which guy I hated worse – the angry screaming Steve or the happy screaming Steve.

True to his word, every week I would get a call from Steve, asking for me personally to make his pizza. Never again did I make it with the secret slice of mozzarella, and never again did he open the pizza inside the store or complain that it didn't look like the picture. He was obnoxious and bothersome, but he ordered every week, and never again did I have to deal with him as a complaint.

I transferred to another store a few months later – and Steve transferred with me! Eventually I moved to a store much too far away, and never heard from him again, but I have to admit I always wondered who ended up with custody of Steve.

First, let's agree that Steve was unreasonable. His complaint, though technically correct, was pointless. Steve became, however, what I call the ULTRA-LOYAL CUSTOMER - *ULC*. The fact that I never again had to prove myself is the most important factor. To an ULTRA-LOYAL CUSTOMER, once you prove yourself, they have faith in you, they trust you. You become insulated from minor errors, insulated from price wars or from the lure of other places; if there is a problem, you can be assured they will come to you calmly and with an eye toward resolution, because the person already knows you will listen, you will try, you will find a solution. Steve is an extreme example (though a completely true story), but the philosophy applies to all customers --- once you create an ultra-loyal customer, you create a solid relationship that you most likely keep for many, many years.

What are the raw materials for ULC's? Occasionally you can create them from your regular customer base, your current customers. However, the best place to find and create ULC's is by bringing back your lost customers. ULC's are created when problems are solved, and many of your lost customers had problems! If you can approach them, bring them back to you, show them that you care, that you listen, that if a problem occurs you will fix it, you will find a large number of people coming back, not just as customers, but as ULTRA-LOYAL CUSTOMERS.

There are occasions where you have to draw a line – where you decide having that person as a customer isn't worth the cost or the aggravation. Only you can decide when that line has been reached – but too many pizza owners reach it too soon.

THE BIG PICTURE

Let's say you have two stores, and in them you have two competent managers. Manager A does sales of about $10,000/week and gives you a net profit of 15%. Manager B does about $12,000, but only gives you a net profit of 13%. Which manager is doing the better job, if all you have to base your decision are these numbers? Most chain pizzerias would immediately say that Manager A is doing the better job, hands down. After all, his food cost must be lower; his labor costs must be lower. He's "controlling." However, at the end of the year, Manager B has brought in an extra $104,000 in sales, and an extra $3,120 in profit right in your pocket. How can it be said he's not doing the better job?

The example is an oversimplification, of course. A hundred factors go into evaluating a manager. My point is that as important as controllables are – and you'll never hear me say that they aren't important – at the end of the week what you as the owner put in your pocket is what you have to spend, and focusing on controllables alone is a sure way to make sure you don't have as much to put in there.

When I worked for a very large pizza chain some years ago as a manager, I was given a store that had lagged in sales for a long time. Profits were often slim or none at the end of the period. I had proven myself able to build sales, and had proven myself competent (though not exceptional) at controlling costs. At this time the company was experiencing a distinct downward trend in sales in the metropolitan area in which I worked – times were not great, and the store I inherited was not busy or profitable. I went into this store with the most gung-ho attitude toward raising sales that anyone could have, and the company gave me a chance to prove that my ideas were worthwhile. I was aggressive, I was creative – in fact, many of the ideas set forth in this book, those came from that period in my career.

When the first P&L statement came out, I was devastated. I had been hoping to give them the biggest profit in that store's history, but instead we had lost $4000. That was $3000 more than they had lost before I arrived. Whether or not I was to be fired I wasn't sure, but I was not looking forward to the visit from my area supervisor.

That afternoon, I saw something worse: the Area Director and his boss, the Regional Director – my boss's boss and his boss – pulled up out front. I was already mentally packing my bags when they walked in the door. I expected something to be said – I didn't expect congratulations and an award! In my shock I even pointed out, "but I lost $4,000 last month!" to which they replied, "Yes, but you've proven in the past that you can control costs. You raised sales $10,000 over the same period last year. This is a business of long term relationships, and you've laid a terrific foundation for long-term profitability."

At the time, though happy, I didn't understand the full impact of what they were telling me, but over the next 22 weeks my store was up in sales every week as compared to the previous year. It was not just the *only* store in the area to be up 22 consecutive weeks, it was often the only store in the metropolitan area to be up at all for a given week. I quickly brought costs under control, and gave the company its best profits for that store.

This is not just a pat-myself-on-the-back story, nor am I suggesting that you shouldn't worry about costs. However, if I had gone into that store and concentrated on percentages over sales, only done those thing which would immediately impact the percentages instead of doing the things I believed would raise sales, I not only wouldn't have been able to raise the sales to that extent, it is possible I would have been able to raise them at all. It is almost impossible to control costs through cutting beyond a certain point – somewhere, by doing that, you sacrifice quality or service, and you'll quickly become a .250 hitter. What you can do, however, is concentrate on raising your sales to cover the costs you need to use to service the customers and provide whatever quality, atmosphere, or special ingredient that makes someone visit you. If you're spending $3000 in labor on $12,000/week in sales, and 25% labor is too high for your bottom line; sure, you can cut the labor back to $2400 (20%) for the week, but do you really think that saving the $600 in labor is going to give you a dramatic increase in profits at the end of the year, especially since now you're running a skeleton crew, increasing their stress levels, reducing their energy levels, and cutting their hours to the point where they consider other jobs? What if you maintained the $3000/week in labor and instead concentrated on using that labor to raise your sales from $12,000 to $15,000, giving you the 20% labor you wanted, but adding all that extra sales and profit to your bottom line?

In short: ***DON'T AUTOMATICALLY LOWER THE LABOR COSTS TO MEET YOUR GOAL, SEE IF YOU CAN RAISE YOUR SALES TO JUSTIFY WHAT YOU SPEND.***

I can almost hear someone reading this and saying "Easier said than done, Rich. Raising sales isn't that easy." No, it's not – raising sales is simple, but it's not easy. Let me ask you this – how easy will it be to raise sales with fewer people working to do it? Cutting labor past a certain point not only eliminates the chance to raise sales, it often creates difficulty in just maintaining them. Suddenly you're struggling to keep at the same level, and looking to cut further. It is a downward spiral that may never end. Raising sales to justify what you spend creates higher profits.

	BASE EXAMPLE	LOWER COST TO MEET GOAL	RAISE SALES TO JUSTIFY COSTS
SALES/WEEK	$12,000	$12,000	$15,000
FOOD/PAPER COST (30%)	$3600	$3600	$4500
LABOR COST (GOAL 20%)	$3000	$2400	$3000
MARKETING	$200	$200	$500
FIXED COSTS	$3400	$3400	$3400
NET PROFIT	$1800	$2400	$3600
YEAR LONG	$93,600	$124,800	$187,200

(Use of the food and labor cost percentages are just round-number examples – yours may be much higher or lower.)

You'll notice that even with the higher labor costs, the higher food cost dollars, and the increased marketing costs, when you have higher sales you not only cover those costs, but you exceed them. Your fixed costs remain the same, so a higher percentage of each sales dollar goes to the bottom line. Don't let that middle column fool you either – for the purposes of being conservative I used the same sales figure even though I cut the labor

94

by $600 – you might not be able to maintain those sales with the reduced labor.

We're not talking about refusing to eliminate wasted time or labor dollars that are completely unnecessary. I'm not advocating people standing around doing nothing or being in any way inefficient. The point I am making is that a sales upswing will help you met your goals much better than a cost reduction, and in the end, put a lot more money in your pocket.

WHAT IS YOUR POTENTIAL?

❑ Take the best week you ever did;
❑ Double it;
❑ Add $100/week for each competitor you have.

That will give you an idea.

PRODUCTIVITY THROUGH PEOPLE

So much of business training is full of phrases that sound like clichés, but this is one that no competent businessperson could argue: your most valuable asset is your crew. It's a simple fact of the business – you cannot take all the orders, make all the pizzas, deliver the entire product line. In fact, you can't accomplish more than a very small percentage of it alone. What you need to get done you get done through others, and what they accomplish depends on the training you give them, in the environment that makes it work. The CYCLE OF PRODUCTIVITY THROUGH PEOPLE is a training model, but one which really doesn't talk about how you train anyone to do anything. All the knowledge in the world, combined with the ability to explain, demonstrate, and evaluate the performance of any employee, amounts to nothing unless you've created an environment where it can be put to use for the benefit of both you AND THE EMPLOYEE. Most training models, you see, talk about the best way to benefit the store, which is fine, except the employee isn't thinking just about the benefit to the store, he/she is thinking about how it impacts him/her – and that's natural. If you want true improvement in any area – most of which has to take place when you are away from the store – then the people must not only be willing and able, but excited, about performing that way, and that means seeing the benefits to them.

It doesn't matter where you start. If you start by paying more then you will, if you hire well, attract better people, and from better people you can expect more. If you can't attract the better people you're looking for, you can – and should – still expect more. Most of the time when you have high standards and set lofty goals you achieve better results, and with better results you can make more money. Wherever you start, each factor feeds into the next, and as long as the pattern is maintained, you reap the benefits.

A young teacher was starting her first full school year in the fifth grade. She was nervous, and was thankful for any advice she could get from the more experienced staff. A few days before school began she asked the other fifth grade teacher how she knew which children needed more attention, which children could handle the harder work, and which children had to be allowed to develop at a slower pace. The other teacher was only too glad to offer some wisdom.

"The first thing I do," she said, "is look closely at the IQ tests the school district conducts each year. Those students who are well above average in intelligence will certainly be able to handle harder work, and those below average – well, you do the best you can for them, but don't expect too much."

Armed with this knowledge the teacher faced the school year more confidently, the students' names and scores always handy inside her top desk drawer. This system made the job much easier, and when the first report cards came out, she was gratified to see that the grades followed very closely the IQ scores – that is, those with high IQ scores received A's and B's, despite the harder and greater amount of work she gave them, and the students with low IQ scores received mostly C's and D's, even though she didn't push them as hard. She felt relieved, she had done her job as well as it could be done.

97

Later that day she met the other fifth grade teacher, and had to thank her for the advice given many weeks ago. She explained how the scores had helped her all through the year, and how the results matched so perfectly. The veteran teacher gave her a confused look, and finally interrupted.

"But that's impossible. Due to budget cuts there were no IQ tests given this year."

"Oh, yes – at least there were for my class. Let me show you." The two teachers walked to the classroom, where the rookie teacher pulled out the paper she had used since the beginning of the year.

"See? Here are the scores, and I must say how thankful I was to have them, because they predicted the abilities of the student wonderfully."

"Oh, dear," the other teacher replied. "You have the list of the students' locker numbers!"

Too often, in business as well as in life, we get what we expect from people.

In my early days of management, one spring I had a chance to work with a very young man named John. John was a shy eighteen-year-old, and this was his first full-time job. Although John was eager and seemingly intelligent, he was a quiet boy, shy and not very assertive. The store was busy, fast-paced and stressful. John wasn't *up to* handling this store, so for weeks on end he mopped floors, took out the trash, and chopped produce. Not much changed over the summer, and John became increasingly unhappy and solitary. He wasn't up to the job, obviously. When the new school year started, suddenly more than the expected number of young employees disappeared, and John was among the few experienced people left. Until we could find someone capable we needed the "body," so we gave John more demanding tasks.

As you might expect with this story, John was more than we had given him credit for. In six months he was a manager, and a year later the General Manager of the store. He went on to spend the next 15 years moving up the ladder in the company, while those who refused to believe he was capable of complex or challenging tasks languished or left.

Not all people rise to the occasion, but many rare coins are left lying on the sidewalk because, from a distance, they look like dirty pennies.

There are two critical rules to PRODUCTIVITY THROUGH PEOPLE:

1. It doesn't matter where you start, as long as you let everyone know the rules and the results.
2. Don't change the rules!

GET A

JUST HAVE YOUR PIZZA ORDER DELIVERED
MON SEPT. 13TH   THROUGH WED. SEPT. 15TH
AND WE'LL BRING YOU A CERTIFICATE FOR A
FREE ROUND 12" PIZZA WITH TWO TOPPINGS
GOOD ANY TIME THIS WEEK (SEPT. 14-19)!

HALL OF FAME
PIZZA & GRILL

DELIVERY
OPEN 7 DAYS
4 PM - 11 PM
WYANDOTTE
ALLEN PARK
MORE

313-333-3333

A SHORT SALES PITCH

If you've read this far – the entire book – then you believe there's merit to my system and that it can help you raise your sales dramatically. But now what? You might have *the time*, the talent, the creativity, *the time*, the desire and *the time* to put this program into play yourself. If so, go for it, and just let me know how it works for you. However, you might not have *the time*, you might not feel you have the skills, and you might not have the desire to do all this yourself. That's okay – I will help you define who your customers are; I will help you emphasize your USP (Unique Selling Point); I will help you figure out how to bring those people in! Anything I can do by phone, through conversation, by reviewing your materials and offering my opinions is free – always!

Need more?

Send me your menus and your current marketing materials. Tell me about your store, your customers, your neighborhood, and your competition. If you can send me menus and marketing from the competition, so much the better! I'll create all the original materials you need, with at least 3 variations of each so you can choose what you like best. I'll send you hard-copy masters, a CD with all materials in multiple formats. These ad pieces are yours to keep for all time, to use without copyright or royalties of any kind. Also, for two years I'll change, edit, revised, or completely recreate new pieces for you. COST: $150

Because you bought my book (and are therefore one of my favorite people in the world) if there's any way I can help, just let me know.

OR - If you want me to come to you and work the two-week program start-to-finish, let's talk about it – anything is possible!

CALL ME

906-369-0793

18443377R00058

Made in the USA
Lexington, KY
04 November 2012